TABLE OF CONTENTS

Sensei Says	1
Tai Chi - The Ultimate Exercise	7
The Power Within - Core Stability in Martial Arts	11
Maxwell Montieth - An Australian Champion	15
Women Warriors	17
The Kyokushinkai	20
How Long Must Your Sleep	27
Real Kung Fu: Debunking the Myths of Kung Fu in China	34
Achieving Mastery Through Kaizen	47
When is it Time to Hang up your Belt	53
Teaching Yourself Hidden Techniques: Bunkai	58
Taking Care of Hamstrings	64
An Equation for Excellence	66
Respect in the Dojo: The Cornerstone of MA Culture	70
Raising the Bar in Coaching	77
The Walking Warrior	80
The Science Behind all Fighting Techniques	87
Issues Facing Women in Martial Arts	90
Mindfulness: Sharpening the Minds Edge	93

Dear Readers,

Welcome to this issue of Martial Arts Australia Magazine. As I sit down to write this letter, I find myself reflecting on the profound journey we all undertake as practitioners of martial arts.

In this issue, I'd like to focus on something that goes beyond techniques and training regimens. I want to discuss the core values that make martial arts not just a method of self-defence or physical fitness, but a path to personal growth and societal improvement.

Let's begin with mindfulness. In our fast-paced world, the ability to be present in the moment is invaluable. On the mats, mindfulness isn't just beneficial—it's essential. It sharpens our focus, enhances our learning, and quite literally keeps us safe during training. But the real power of mindfulness lies in how we carry it into our daily lives. Imagine approaching every challenge with the same focused awareness we bring to our martial arts practice. The potential for personal growth and positive impact is enormous.

Equally important is the concept of respect. In the dojo, respect goes far beyond the formal rituals of bowing or addressing instructors by their proper titles. It's about recognising the value in every person you train with, from the newest beginner to the most experienced practitioner. It's understanding that everyone has something to teach us if we approach our training with humility and openness.

We must also acknowledge the crucial role our instructors play. These dedicated individuals commit their lives to passing on their knowledge, often motivated by little more than the satisfaction of seeing their students grow. Showing them respect means more than adhering to dojo etiquette; it's about truly valuing their guidance and repaying their dedication with our own commitment to learning and growth.

These values—mindfulness, respect, humility—are not confined to martial arts. They are fundamental to building a better society.

Consider how our communities might change if we approached every interaction with the respect we show our training partners, every conversation with the mindfulness we bring to our forms, every challenge with the perseverance we demonstrate when learning a difficult technique. The potential for positive change is immense.

In martial arts, we're not just training our bodies or learning self-defence. We're cultivating values that can transform our lives and the lives of those around us. We're developing tools to become better friends, colleagues, and community members.

As the renowned martial artist and philosopher Bruce Lee once said, "Knowledge will give you power, but character respect." In our dojos, we're building both knowledge and character. This holistic development is something we should all be proud of and strive to continue.

As you read through this issue, I encourage you to remember this: the true power of martial arts lies not in the strength of our strikes or the complexity of our techniques, but in the strength of our character and the depth of our respect for others.

Let us commit to training diligently, practicing mindfulness, and always showing respect. This is the true way of the martial artist, and it's a path that can lead us to become not just better practitioners, but better human beings.

Yours sincerely
Vanessa McKay

All content published in MAMA (Marital Arts Magazine Australia), including articles, images, and other media, is the property of the magazine and is protected by copyright law. The author retains the copyright to their individual work, but by submitting their work to MAMA, they grant the magazine an exclusive, perpetual, and irrevocable license to publish and distribute their work in all formats, including print, digital, and online media. No part of MAMA may be reproduced, distributed, or transmitted in any form or by any means, including photocopying, recording, or other electronic or mechanical methods, without the prior written permission of the magazine.

MAMA respects the intellectual property rights of others and expects its contributors and readers to do the same. If you believe that your copyrighted work has been used in a way that constitutes copyright infringement, please contact MAMA immediately. Additionally, any use of MAMA trademarks, including the magazine's name and logo, without prior written authorization from the magazine, is prohibited.

MAMA strives to showcase original and unique content, and as such, does not accept any submissions that have been previously published or that are under consideration by other publications. By submitting their work to MAWA Magazine, the author confirms that their work is original and has not been published or submitted elsewhere.

In addition, MAMA reserves the right to edit all submissions for grammar, style, and clarity, and to reject any submission that does not adhere to the magazine's standards or guidelines. The magazine also reserves the right to remove or modify any content that is deemed inappropriate or offensive, at its sole discretion.

MAMA acknowledges and respects the rights of all individuals and groups and will not publish any content that promotes hate speech, discrimination, or any form of violence. The magazine also respects the privacy of its contributors and readers and will not share or sell any personal information to third parties without prior written consent. By submitting their work to MAMA, the author agrees to abide by these copyright specifics and to grant the magazine the rights outlined in this statement. The author also certifies that their work is original and does not infringe on the rights of any third party. MAMA reserves the right to modify these copyright specifics at any time without prior notice.

If you have any questions or concerns regarding these copyright specifics, please contact MAMA at info@martialartsmagazineaustralia.com

Sensei Says....

I started training with a friend of mine and at first it was great we were both learning together but I have started to take my journey more seriously, I want to grade up the ranks and maybe teach someday. He on the other hand is happy to slack off and talk through training, it annoys me and i am afraid it will ruin our friendship

I understand your concern, and it's a situation that many martial artists encounter during their journey. Balancing friendship with the pursuit of personal goals in martial arts can be challenging. Here are some steps you can consider:

- Open Communication: Sit down with your friend and have an open, honest conversation about your respective goals and expectations. Express your passion for martial arts and your desire to advance, possibly to a teaching level. Ensure your friend understands the importance of your commitment.
- Set Boundaries: Establish training boundaries together. Let your friend know that when it's time to train, you expect a focused and disciplined approach. Make it clear that there is a time and place for socializing, but during training, your primary focus is on learning and progressing.
- Lead by Example: Demonstrate your dedication through consistent effort, discipline, and progress. Your dedication may inspire your friend to take training more seriously. Be a positive role model in your training sessions.
- Find Common Ground: Identify areas where you can both benefit from training together. Explore shared interests or goals that align with your training sessions, which can keep the friendship intact while still allowing for progress.
- Seek Additional Training Partners: If your friend's approach consistently hinders your progress and causes frustration, consider seeking additional training partners or joining a class where you can surround yourself with individuals who share your level of commitment.
- Maintain Perspective: Remember that martial arts is a personal journey, and each person progresses at their own pace. While your paths may diverge in training intensity, it doesn't have to negatively impact your friendship if you communicate openly and respect each other's choices.

Ultimately, the key is finding a balance that allows you to pursue your martial arts goals while maintaining a positive relationship with your friend. It may take time and effort, but with clear communication and mutual understanding, you can navigate this situation successfully.

Help! children are ruining my training sessions. I am in the beginners class at my karate class and there are quite a few children in the class, they alway muck up and slow the pace of the class. I understand that we are a small club but how can I encourage them to behave without looking like an 'asshole' I need my training time too.

It's understandable that you want to make the most of your training sessions, but it's important to approach this situation with empathy and consideration for the children and their parents. Here are some steps you can take to address the issue without coming across as harsh:

- Talk to the Instructor: Start by discussing your concerns with your karate instructor privately. Share your perspective on how the children's behavior is affecting your training experience. In many cases, instructors are already aware of such issues and can make adjustments or provide guidance.
- Offer to Assist: If you feel comfortable and have the skills to do so, offer to assist the instructor during certain parts of the class. This could involve helping the younger students with their techniques, keeping them engaged, or even demonstrating proper behavior and focus.
- Talk to the Parents: If appropriate, have a respectful conversation with the parents of the children involved. Express your concern in a non-confrontational manner, focusing on how their children's behavior affects the overall quality of the class for everyone.

- Suggest Separate Classes: If your club has enough members, you could suggest the idea of having separate classes for adults and children, especially if the age and skill gap is significant. This would allow both groups to train at their own pace without hindering each other's progress.
- Lead by Example: During training, set a positive example by demonstrating focus, discipline, and respect for the instructor and fellow students. Your dedication can inspire others, including the children, to follow suit.
- Supportive Encouragement: When you notice a child making an effort or behaving well, offer words of encouragement and praise. This can reinforce positive behavior and create a more cooperative atmosphere.
- Patience and Understanding: Remember that children are still learning and may not fully grasp the expectations of a karate class. Try to exercise patience and understanding, recognizing that they too are there to learn and grow.
- Seek Alternatives: If you find that the situation doesn't improve and it significantly impacts your training, consider discussing alternative training options with your instructor, such as private lessons or advanced classes.

Approaching the issue with empathy, open communication, and a willingness to collaborate with both the instructor and parents can help create a more harmonious training environment for everyone involved.

Finding time for training while juggling work, family, and other commitments is challenging. How can I maintain a consistent training schedule without neglecting other aspects of my life?

In the fast-paced rhythm of modern life, finding time for martial arts training can be a Herculean task. Juggling work, family, and other commitments often leaves us feeling like tightrope walkers, desperately seeking balance. Yet, maintaining a consistent training schedule is not only possible but also essential for personal growth and well-being. In this article, we'll explore practical strategies to help you carve out time for your martial arts journey without neglecting other crucial aspects of your life.

Prioritising and Goal Setting:
The first step in mastering the delicate art of balancing training with life commitments is to set clear priorities and goals. Understand the role martial arts plays in your life—whether it's a form of exercise, stress relief, or personal development. By identifying your priorities, you can allocate time more effectively and ensure that your training aligns with your overall life goals.

Time Management Techniques:
Effective time management is the linchpin of maintaining a consistent training schedule. Consider implementing time-blocking techniques, where specific blocks of time are dedicated to different activities. Create a weekly schedule that includes designated time slots for work, family, and, of course, martial arts training. Stick to these time blocks as closely as possible to establish a routine that accommodates all facets of your life.

Early Mornings and Late Evenings:
For many individuals, the early morning or late evening hours provide golden opportunities for uninterrupted training sessions. Consider waking up an hour earlier to hit the dojo or practice at home before the day begins. Alternatively, use the quiet hours after everyone else has gone to bed. These time slots not only offer solitude but also set a positive tone for the day or provide a relaxing conclusion to your evening.

Incorporate Family Time:
Integrating martial arts into your family life can be a creative way to spend quality time together while staying committed to your training. Explore family-friendly martial arts activities or encourage your loved ones to join you in light workouts. This not only fosters a supportive environment but also instils a sense of shared accomplishment and well-being.

Efficient Training Sessions:
Recognise that the duration of your training sessions doesn't always dictate their effectiveness. Focus on quality

rather than quantity. Design workouts that maximise your time and target specific goals. High-intensity interval training (HIIT) and focused, goal-oriented practices can provide substantial benefits in shorter time frames.

Combining Work and Training:
If workable, explore opportunities to integrate martial arts into your work routine. Some workplaces offer fitness facilities or allow employees to take short breaks for physical activity. Incorporating brief stretching or movement exercises during work hours can contribute to your overall fitness and provide a mental refresher.

Open Communication:
Clear communication with your family, employer, and training partners is crucial. Discuss your commitment to martial arts and the importance it holds in your life. By expressing your goals and schedule openly, you create understanding and may even garner support from those around you.

Flexibility and Adaptability:
Life is inherently unpredictable, and rigid schedules can crumble in the face of unexpected challenges. Embrace flexibility and develop the ability to adapt your training routine when necessary. This adaptability ensures that occasional disruptions don't derail your entire plan, allowing you to bounce back quickly and maintain consistency in the long run.

Self-Care and Recovery:
While committing to regular training is essential, so is prioritising self-care and recovery. Over training can lead to burnout and compromise your ability to manage life's demands effectively. Incorporate rest days into your routine, listen to your body, and ensure that your training enhances, rather than hinders, your overall well-being.

Balancing martial arts training with the myriad responsibilities of life is undeniably challenging, but it's a challenge worth embracing. By setting priorities, managing time effectively, and fostering open communication, you can strike a harmonious balance between your training and the other facets of your life. Remember, the journey is as important as the destination, and finding equilibrium is a continuous process that evolves as you grow both as a martial artist and as an individual.

I get extremely nervous before competitions, affecting my performance. Do you have any tips for managing pre-competition stress and staying focused?

Competing in martial arts can be a thrilling and rewarding experience, but the anxiety that precedes competitions is a common hurdle many practitioners face. Pre-competition nervousness can significantly impact performance, hindering the ability to showcase one's skills effectively. In this article, we'll delve into practical tips and strategies to help martial artists manage pre-competition stress, stay focused, and step onto the mat with confidence.

Before exploring coping strategies, it's essential to recognise that feeling nervous before a competition is entirely normal. In fact, a certain level of nervousness can be beneficial, as it signifies a heightened state of alertness and readiness. The key is to manage these nerves in a way that enhances performance rather than detracts from it.

Mental Preparation:
Adequate mental preparation is fundamental in managing pre-competition stress. Visualisation techniques can be powerful tools to create a mental image of success. Spend time mentally rehearsing your techniques, imagining yourself executing flawless moves with precision. This not only reinforces muscle memory, but also instils a sense of confidence in your abilities.

Breathing Exercises:
Controlled breathing is a proven method of managing stress and anxiety. Implement deep breathing exercises, focusing on slow inhalations and exhalations. Practice diaphragmatic breathing to calm the nervous system and centre your mind. Incorporate these exercises into your pre-competition routine to establish a sense of tranquillity.

Progressive Muscle Relaxation (PMR):
Tension often accompanies nervousness, leading to physical tightness and diminished performance. Progressive Muscle Relaxation (PMR) is a technique where you systematically tense and then release each muscle group in your body. This process helps alleviate physical tension, promoting a state of relaxation. Practice PMR during your warm-up or in the moments leading up to your competition.

Establish a Routine:
Create a pre-competition routine that encompasses both physical and mental aspects. Engage in familiar warm-up exercises and rituals that bring a sense of normalcy to the competition environment. Establishing a routine signals to your brain that it's time to transition into competition mode, minimising the impact of anxiety.

Positive Affirmations:
The power of positive affirmations should not be underestimated. Develop a set of affirmations that resonate with you and focus on your strengths and capabilities. Repeat these affirmations before and during the competition to shift your mindset from anxiety to empowerment.

Focus on the Process, Not the Outcome:
Redirect your attention from the potential outcomes of the competition to the process itself. Concentrate on executing each technique flawlessly, staying present in the moment. By shifting your focus to the task at hand, you mitigate the overwhelming pressure associated with the end result.

Pre-Competition Routine:
Craft a pre-competition routine that includes activities you find calming and enjoyable.

PWhether it's listening to music, engaging in light stretching, or reading a motivational quote, these rituals can serve as comforting anchors in the midst of pre-competition nerves.

Utilise Arousal Control:
Understand the concept of arousal control, which involves regulating the level of excitement and energy before a competition. Experiment with techniques to either increase or decrease arousal based on your individual needs. Some may benefit from energetic activities to raise arousal, while others might find calm activities more effective.

Seek Professional Guidance:
If pre-competition anxiety becomes overwhelming and persistent, consider seeking guidance from a sports psychologist or mental performance coach. These professionals specialise in helping athletes develop coping strategies, manage stress, and optimise their mental state for peak performance.

Learn from Experience:

Each competition provides an opportunity to learn more about yourself and your reactions to stress. After each event, reflect on your experiences—what worked, what didn't, and how you can improve your pre-competition routine. This reflective practice contributes to ongoing personal growth and enhanced performance in future competitions.

Pre-competition stress is a shared experience among martial artists, but with the right strategies, it can be managed effectively. By incorporating mental preparation, breathing exercises, relaxation techniques, and positive affirmations into your routine, you can transform pre-competition nerves into a source of strength and focus. Remember, the journey to mastering pre-competition jitters is as individual as your martial arts practice, and finding the right combination of strategies may require some experimentation. With perseverance and a proactive mindset, you can step onto the competition mat with confidence, ready to showcase your skills and embrace the thrill of the martial arts journey.

Mantras to try...

Calm mind, strong body.

I am focused and ready.

Each movement is deliberate and powerful.

My training guides me to victory.

I respect my opponent and honor the art.

I am centered, balanced, and in control.

My spirit is unbreakable.

I adapt and overcome all challenges.

With every breath, I grow stronger.

I embody discipline and perseverance.

Choose one or more that resonate with you, and repeat it often.

Have you ever wondered what that exercise is you see people doing in the parks so early in the mornings? It's called Tai Chi and it's been around for centuries. So why is it still relatively unknown, and how can moving slowly be good exercise for you?

Tai Chi is a set of movements that are performed slowly in order to promote good health.
Originating in China centuries ago, this ancient art literally translated means the "Supreme Ultimate" and its main purpose was specifically designed for self defence in the martial arts.

Martial artists of that period were constantly in search for a fighting style that was undefeatable or the "ultimate" fighting style. What they discovered, was that the more relaxed you were during a fight, your thoughts were clear and free from emotional anger thus, being able to respond to attacks more appropriately giving you the upper hand over an opponent whose judgement was clouded by anger.

So in order to train the body to be more relaxed during fighting, they practised techniques slowly. This relaxed the muscles from tensing up and slowed the breathing down to lower the heart rate. Whether it was intentional or not, they discovered many other benefits to one's health improved through this type of training.

These days, Tai Chi is practised mainly because of the significant health benefits it has to offer. Here are some of those benefits and how it works.

Weight Loss
Fitness professionals will recommend higher intensity exercises such as running to burn more calories faster. A typical one hour Tai Chi session can burn somewhere between 280-300 calories. Simply put, if you're moving, your burning calories. If you're burning calories, you're contributing to weight loss.

Fitness
Tai Chi gets you to work on special breathing techniques that help cultivate your 'Qi' or 'Chi' energy throughout your body. Any kind of breath work is essentially using your heart and lungs which are the main organs used to improve your cardio-respiratory system.

Stress Relief, Focus and Concentration
Tai Chi requires you to move slowly and keep your body relaxed. Moving in such a way gives you the sensation as what can be best described as 'moving meditation'. When moving in a meditative like state, your mind has to concentrate as well as be totally aware of every minute move.

Ailments and Diseases
As mentioned earlier, Tai Chi movements are designed to cultivate 'Qi' to flow freely throughout the body. If there is an interruption to this 'flow', this is believed to be the cause of sickness both mental

and physical. Tai Chi aims to balance the flow of 'Qi'.

Energy Levels
After a Tai Chi session, you will feel totally relaxed and energised. A combination of mind and body exercise, you are left feeling good about yourself, not only physically, but mentally as well.

Confidence and Relationships
When you feel good about yourself, you will discover a new sense of confidence which can lead you into interacting with people around you more positively.

Tai Chi should be practised with full heartedness and sincerity. It is a harmonious combination of art and exercise that provides a deeper level of self knowledge and spiritual harmony. With constant practice, one will soon find balance and understand their place in the universe.

Tai Chi: Fundamental Principles to Practicing Tai Chi.

This section of the article intends to give a brief guide on the fundamentals of Tai Chi practice before commencing.

Now that we have a bit of a deeper understanding on the benefits Tai Chi has to offer, let us now look at a few essential principles that need to be applied when starting any Tai Chi program.

To gain all the benefits and understand Tai Chi in all its glory, takes time, dedication, patience and consistency with your practice. Many time as a beginner, you may expect to achieve your goals in your very first lesson. It should be understood, that the chances of this happening is unlikely and that you should not let it deter you from practicing. Tai Chi is a very deep and multi-faceted art that requires much practice to achieve your desired objectives. However, if you can understand and apply some of the following principles, you can expect to reach your goals sooner.

Rising to the top
This refers to your spirit. When performing Tai Chi movements, you should keep your head upright firm but relaxed. Do not allow tension to come in as this will block the flow of energy. The best way to gauge the correct technique is to look where you eye line level is. Try not to look down at your toes or higher than your head. When you rise your spirit to the top, you will attain a state of mental freshness.

Lower the chest, raise the back
A simple way to practice this principle, is to think of caving in your chest and rounding your shoulders forward while keeping your back straight. Just be mindful to keep your body relaxed without any tension. Again this will allow the energy to flow more freely throughout your body.

Loosen the waist
All your movements are driven from the waist which is the controlling part of the torso. Keeping your waist supple will relax the upper body movements while maintaining a strong stable stance.

Differentiate between 'Apparent' and 'Solid'
When you place all your body weight one leg (solid) and counter support your balance with the leg that has no body weight on it (apparent), you will have a better understanding of how to make your movements more agile when stepping.

Sink shoulders, drop elbows
To understand this feeling, stand upright and imagine hugging an invisible beach ball against your chest. Now if your shoulders are tense and your elbows are high, simple exhale slowly and watch how they sink. Notice how your upper body suddenly becomes more relaxed.

Use will, not strength
One way to interpret this is to let your mind be focused and concentrate on the movements to come out as naturally as possible without forcing it. Again, the objective here is to get your body to relax using the power of the mind.

Coordination between top and bottom
An easy way to think of this is to make sure that your upper body movements are coordinated with your lower body's. Not just hands and feet, but also the waist, shoulders, torso. Even the eyes and breathing must be unified together so that they all start moving together and finish moving together for any given move. This is the essence of 'Yin-Yang harmony'.

Internal and external unity
Again we look at the concept of yin-yang theory being applied to movements between the mind and the body. Essentially, if your movement is extended or 'open' then so should your mind be. Likewise, if your movement is drawn in your mind should be 'closed' or more focused.

Continuity without break
When performing a set of combined movements of a Tai Chi routine, each and every individual move should link to each other as if they were one long continuous movement rather than many separate ones.

Seeking stillness in movement
When you slow movements down, your breathing will naturally become deep and long. The body is more relaxed and then there will be no blockages to allow the energy to flow freely throughout the body. The slower the movements the better, almost to the point where it feels as if you are not moving at all.

Applying these principles is one of the first step to your success in Tai Chi practice. You may also come across some styles of Tai Chi that may look different in their but all of them should share these essential principles. One of the main purposes in the correct use of the fundamentals is to help the practitioner cultivate 'chi' energy which can be considered the life force that helps regulate our well being.

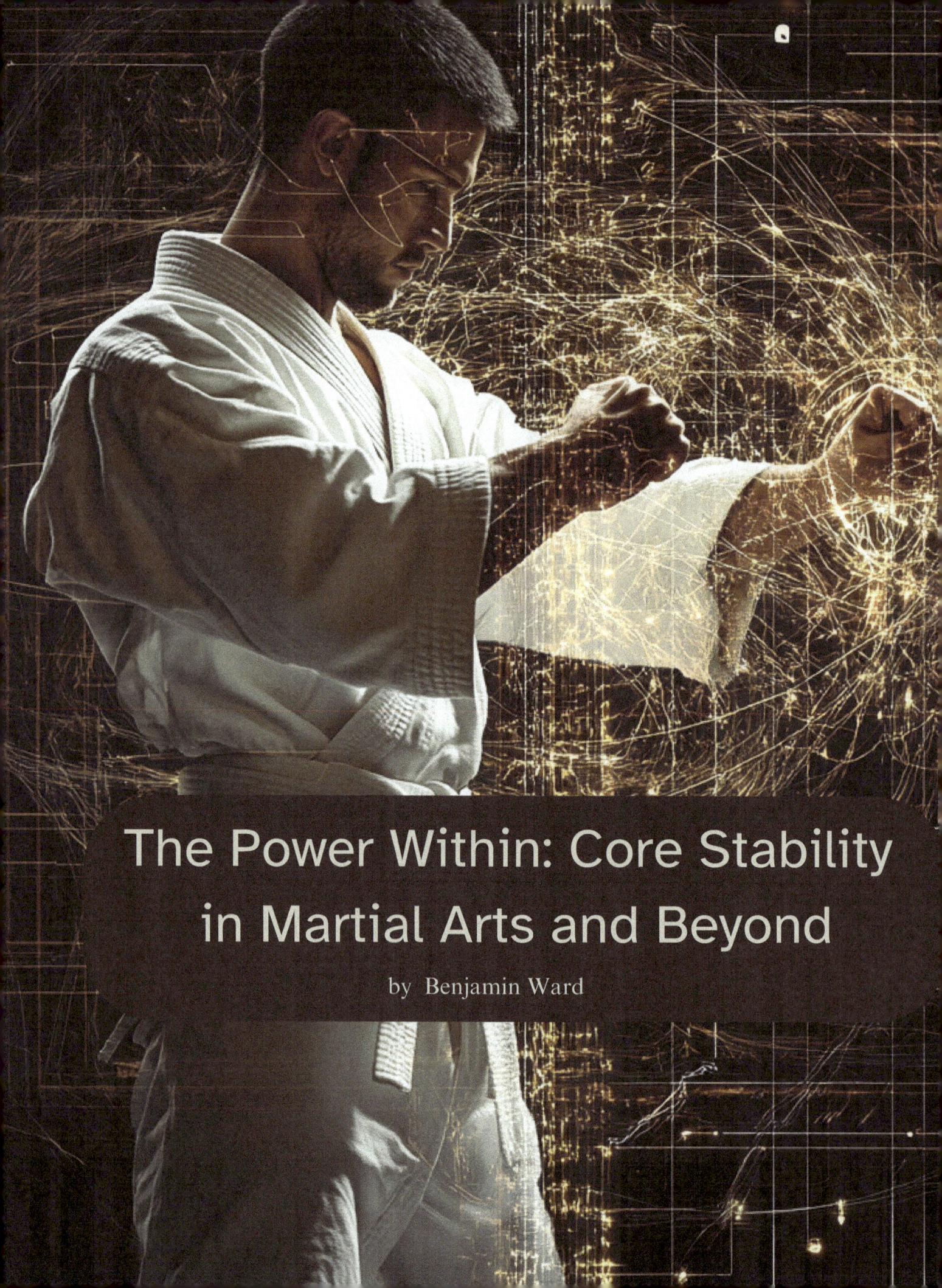

"Proximal stability enhances distal athleticism and power," as Dr Stuart McGill aptly puts it. This principle, deeply ingrained in traditional martial arts, has recently found its way into modern exercise science, bridging centuries-old wisdom with contemporary research.

In my current exercise science studies at university, I've encountered a fascinating convergence. Our course in exercise prescription, led by a seasoned powerlifter, has been shaped around principles strikingly similar to those I've been taught in my Karate style at Sei Do Kai dojos in Coolum Beach, Sunshine Coast. These theories, championed by Kaicho Branko Russan and Kokoro John Core, form the bedrock of our training. However, as my instructor Kokoro wisely noted, "You can take a horse to water, but you can't make them drink."

I've observed that many of my young course mates may go on to teach these principles without fully grasping their depth. In their own exercise routines, they'll likely prioritise quantity over quality—a common pitfall of youth—favouring hundreds of repetitions over a few sets of perfect executions. Yet, anyone who has performed a kata correctly even once knows the breathtaking intensity these principles demand when properly applied.

These concepts have profoundly influenced my own weightlifting practice, dramatically increasing the force I can generate and the pressure I can apply through my core.

Interestingly, I recently watched a Cynthia Rothrock film from the early 80s where she instructed a class of coloured belts to 'lock up your body' and 'tense at the impact'. It seems these principles have long been embedded in advanced and traditional karate practice.

While these concepts go by many names and I hesitate to oversimplify the nuanced instruction in dojos worldwide —I'll attempt to elucidate them. Imagine your core as the centre of your body, with your limbs as distal levers connecting to weights or executing techniques. By pulling your ribs down towards your pelvis and tilting your pelvis to a flatter position—what Tai Chi practitioners call 'not tipping the bowl'—you straighten your spine and strengthen your posture.

As you move through various kata or techniques, maintain this strong posture while subtly releasing and contracting it in the areas being moved. This creates and maintains abdominal pressure from the start to the finish of your kata or the execution of a 'one hit, one kill' technique, or "Ikken Hassatsu". The result? A locked core that generates remarkable power and athleticism in your extremities.

This principle aligns with Sherrington's Law of Irradiation, which states that tensing one muscle activates surrounding muscles and amplifies strength in muscles already in use. A simple demonstration: while standing, tense your buttocks, then clench your fists. You'll likely find your buttocks tensing harder.

Paradoxically, this posture and abdominal pressure needn't be maintained at 100% effort constantly. It can be dialled back to 0%, 10%, or 20% conscious effort when moving through techniques requiring greater core flexibility or extreme speed and adjustability. Many kung fu or self-defence techniques work brilliantly because of this adjustability.

In my bodyweight training, I've noticed interesting effects of this principle. Years ago, someone commented on the size of my biceps, which surprised me as I wasn't specifically training them. I realised that in bodyweight exercises, it's nearly impossible to isolate muscle groups. As major muscle groups tire, stabilising muscles take up the slack. During push-ups, for instance, the work shifts from chest to shoulders to triceps, ultimately engaging the entire arm.

I've adapted my push-up technique to leverage core bracing, aiming my core and upper body forward at the chest and scapulas, with the upper back arched. It's almost like performing a dynamic tension double punch into the floor. This technique, refined through dojo training, has significantly enhanced my weightlifting performance.

However, it's worth noting that this intense core bracing isn't necessary for every movement, whether in acrobatic bodyweight training or in the varied techniques of sparring and self-defence.

My powerlifting course coordinator, for instance, doesn't focus much on sit-ups or flexibility training, except for those with very limited ranges of motion. His emphasis is squarely on power development.

While we might not need to consider power development for everyday tasks like carrying groceries or shutting a car door, in martial arts—as in many sports like track and field or NFL—it's crucial. Making these principles of core bracing and posture maintenance second nature when generating force is invaluable, especially when compared to incorrect techniques that might arise from insufficient training.

I've even found these principles useful in unexpected situations. Recently, while recovering from leg surgery, I found myself unconsciously applying core bracing techniques to stabilise my weakened leg during night-time trips to the toilet. By creating tension in my foot and lower leg muscles, I was able to move more safely and confidently.

In conclusion, whether we call it 'core bracing', 'locking up', or 'centrifugal force', this principle of power amplification is fundamental to the 'one hit, one kill' philosophy of Karate. It's akin to Popeye opening his can of spinach or Captain Planet materialising 'when our powers combine'. While it may seem like learning something entirely new, it's really about refining and focusing what you already know.

Finding a teacher who can effectively convey these principles is crucial. Every Karate practitioner must learn to produce the power of 'one hit, one kill', and in my view, mastering these ancient principles of core bracing and abdominal pressure control is the only way to achieve it. It's a journey of consistent practice and revisiting, balancing power with flexibility, as both are integral to the martial arts. And even after years of training, I feel I'm only halfway there.

Maxwell Montieth - An Australian Champion

by
James Heenan

July 2024 sixteen year old Maxwell Montieth was part of the 22 Australian representatives among the 1500 participants at the first championships since the pandemic.

Now known as one of the first Victorians to compete at the World Championships in Korea, Max was initially unsure of his performance, saying that there was never a moment, "I actually thought I was going to win. Even when I made it to the third round I was still thinking i was going to lose."

He adds, " The support I had around me certainly helped, everyone was there to support me and even though I still had the thought [of losing] in the back of my head, I wanted to bring gold back to my family and I just kind of fell into that mindset."

Through excellent swordsmanship, grit and the echoes of his peers' encouragements, Max advanced to the final round where he prevailed against the competition.

Max belonged in the under-18s brown belt category ranked first after the initial gumbup, or forms category. After showcasing various cuts, strikes, blocks and stances, Max became the top-ranking competitor amount 12 others and was set to take on the 12th ranked individual in an elimination tourney.

We are very lucky because Australia came first, equal to South Korea, which is a first ever.

Preparation for the tournament was strenuous for Max, with school being a priority, practice usually happened during late nights, with special session with Grandmaster Jung-II Oh on Tuesdays.

The president of Haidong Gumdo OCeania, Grandmaster Jung-II Oh visited Heenan Taekwondo to train the Australian competitors, something that Max took advantage of leading up to the championships.

The president of Haidong Gumdo OCeania, Grandmaster Jung-II Oh visited Heenan Taekwondo to train the Australian competitors, something that Max took advantage of leading up to the championships.

His training paid off, and even as the gold medal weighs heavy on his neck, the feat to Max is still unbelievable despite his new sense of confidence.

Max showed his abilities during the two day competition retreat, with the wooden swords called bokken used for sparring. They are heavier with more drag than their steel conterparts. A timber sword is llike picking up a tennis racket, you just have to make it work for you.

If you get an official sword, which is assigned to you, it is meant to suit you. You don't get a sword until your are a black belt so you have to make the sword work for you when you are on the timber ones.

With no grips, no sheet or sheath, less balance, more weight and more air displacement Max's performance was very impressive.

As for the key tips he received during the lead up to the final match, keeping his breathing in check was of utmost importance, with Max taking long breaths to maintain his focus.

Max has been training with the sword for nearly two years said that the experience of learning has been amazing and much of it has to do with the community around it.

"I think it teaches you discipline, perseverance and integrity, and I think others should dive in and give it try," he said.

Also a taekwondo practitioner, Max is looking forward to heading to Brisbane later this year to compete.

The team here at Martial Arts Magazine Australia, wish him every success!

James Heenan from Heenan Taekwondo
Phone: 0407 869988

Women Warriors: Martial Artists Sharpen Skills in Port Kennedy WA

Instructors: Marisa Simeone KUA; Meg Croucher Agoge Boxing Gym; Ann Draper Gojo Ryu; Kim Benn KUA; Jenna Sinclair GKR; Tabatha Ingle GKR; Melanie Tuaranga BJJ; Roberta Bobadilla BJJ; Danica Ghozali BJJ.

On October 12, 2024, Port Kennedy, Western Australia, became the epicentre of female martial arts prowess as 48 dedicated practitioners gathered for an intensive 4-hour Women In Martial Arts Workshop. This remarkable event, orchestrated by coordinator Ann Draper, brought together some of Western Australia's finest female martial artists on an equal platform to share their knowledge and passion for various fighting disciplines.

These skilled instructors shared innovative training ideas, offering participants a chance to explore new martial art styles, master intricate fighting combinations, and learn practical self-defense techniques. For many, the workshop provided an exciting opportunity to wield the Bo for the first time.

The workshop featured an impressive lineup of instructors, each bringing their unique expertise to the table.

Anne Draper - Organiser

Ann Draper, the event's coordinator and a 30-year veteran of the Goju Karate Association WA, praised the workshop's success, highlighting the palpable energy and enthusiasm of the participants. "This event will help shape the direction of our training," Draper explained, "making it stronger by strengthening relationships and spreading the vast depth of female martial arts knowledge across different styles."

Beyond the mat, the workshop made a significant impact by directing its proceeds to local charities focused on critical issues:

-RIZEUP Australia: Supporting families impacted by domestic violence

Kai Fella: Suicide prevention initiatives

WARPINE: Research into rare cancer treatments

The day's intense action and camaraderie were beautifully captured by 'Vivid Nostalgia' photography, preserving the memories of this empowering event.

A Team Effort
The success of the workshop was made possible by a dedicated team of instructors and assistants:

For more information about future Women In Martial Arts Workshops, contact Ann Draper at women.inmartialarts1@gmail.com or call 0417 992 019.

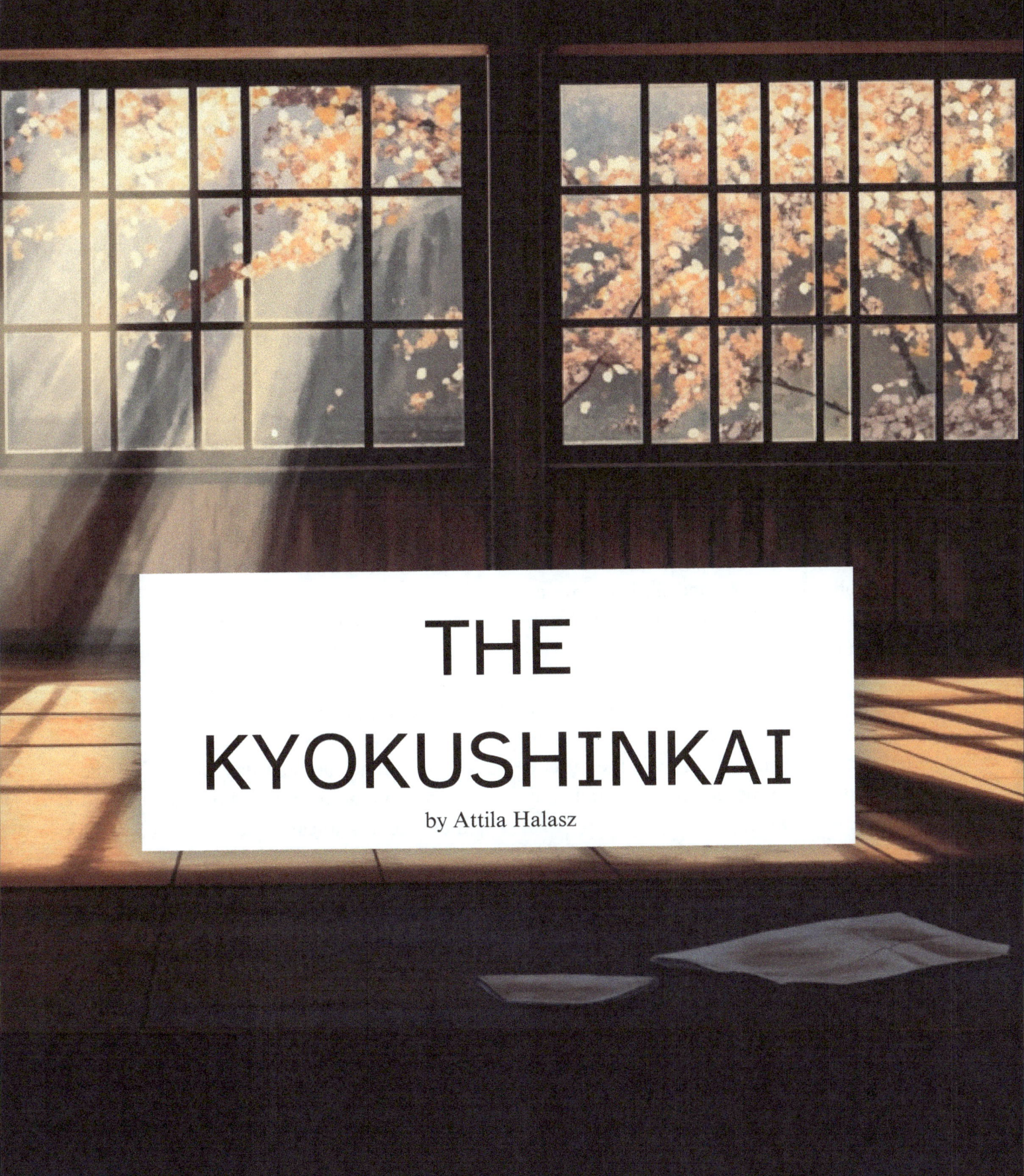

Before Aikido, I was in the Kyokushinkai

The long bus ride from Perth WA to Sydney took nearly four days in 1986. Cheap, short term accommodation was to be found in Western Sydney, but the Kyokushinkai Headquarters were located at Bondi Junction, in the posh Eastern Suburbs.

I was 20 years old, however job opportunities were thin just then, so I commuted every day for karate training to occupy myself.

The Kyokushinkai was the best value martial art in those days. I paid the set fee of $30 for a month for unlimited training. Naturally I turned up for every class wearing my tracksuit. Kids classes, basic classes, advanced classes, kihon-kata-kumite classes, all of them.

Legendary Australian grandmaster, 6th dan John Taylor started noticing me as did his popular head instructor, 2nd dan Jim Phillips.

Seeing me all the time, Shihan Taylor suggested I buy a white Japanese made uniform but I just didn't have the money for it. He gave me one anyway and said to pay, when I can.

After a while he enquired where and how I lived, so I told him.

I actually started struggling with paying rent and when John Taylor heard that he made the most amazing offer:

"Why don't you become the first live-in student, an "uchi deshi" here at HQ until you find a job?- he asked.

I was astonished! I took up his very kind offer immediately.

I actually got my own room next to the training hall. I cleaned the showers and office, swept the dojo, took phone inquiries and trained and trained.

Word got out that there is a live-in student at HQ and black belts started to show up on Sunday to practice fight drills with me and I was happy to assist.

After a Saturday class John Taylor pulled me aside and told me he was expecting a Japanese delegation from Tokyo on Monday. As they will come to the dojo first from the airport, I should spend Sunday cleaning.

Two distinguished black belts, hand picked to teach in Australia by Masutatsu Oyama, the founder himself.
It was exciting news!

I got up late the next day, turned up the music volume on my radio and surveyed the large task ahead.

Suddenly the bell rang.
I thought, whoever black belt that is, I have to send him away because of the upcoming cleaning.
To my surprise, there were two Japanese men standing at the door wearing dark suits and carrying travel luggage.

I invited them in and they looked around in the dojo with great interest, checking out the trophies in the glass cabinet and photos hanging on the wall. I immediately rang John Taylor.

Hi Attila, how is the cleaning going?- he asked with a bright voice.
They are here...the delegation is here- I answered somewhat nervously. That got Shihan nervous too.

He turned up 30 minutes later with his car and drove the two men to their designated hotel...one day early.
I thought well, now that they've already been...a more relaxed Sunday is ahead for me :-) .

The following Wednesday brought my fondest memory of the Bondi Junction Kyokushinkai HQ.

The visiting masters, Sensei Kato and Ishi san held classes together on Monday and Tuesday but for Wednesday a senior student kumite class was announced with all brown and black belts expected to attend the fights.

Kato was a 3rd dan personal student of Oyama and a thunderous, fast fighting machine.

I was a lowly blue belt but as a live in student, I joined the line up anyway for this fight class. I thought I'll be able to survive the full contact round.

After the warm up, Kato walked out to the middle of the room and took up a fighting stance. He made a speech with a heavy Japanese accent about being dedicated and strong in the face of any pain or hardship. He was now ready to assess the attendees, individually.

The fights started with ferocious intensity. Kato was brutal. No student stood a chance, they fell like chess pieces, one after another.

I thought our own Keith was a pretty good fighter but Kato hit him so hard in the chest that he collapsed.

I was the last in line to fight. Kato was told earlier that I'm an uchi deshi...but he wasn't told that I was one out of necessity!

He hit me and kicked me properly like I was a black belt. A roundhouse kick to the head brought me down. I was so dizzy, barely made it back to the line.

Everybody was relieved that the hard fights were over. But Kato was still out in the middle! Insisting on a second round with everyone!

Two fighters flagged injury and didn't stand up, the two females in line also decided not to go.

This second round was even more furious than the first one as Kato was really angry at the lack of the fighting spirit. He probably measured it against his own.

He devastated his fellow assistant, Ishi as well in this round. He was limping back to the line after several, brutal low kicks.

When it was my turn, something came over me. I lunged at Kato with several "Kiai!" shouts, punched and kicked him as hard as I could.

He was a particularly great man. He could have easily kicked me in the head again but he carefully avoided that, instead he pounded my chest so hard with body blows that at one point I couldn't breathe.

Somehow, I survived.

You could feel the relief in the room that it was finally over!

But Kato stayed in the middle. Insisting on a third round!

Maybe he himself was a full time karate student back home but here at Bondi Junction, among us there were bus drivers, uni students, tradies, dentists, who all had work the next day.

There was a reluctant silence. People nursed their injuries and clearly had enough.

The moment of no motion grew really long and awkward.

I read enough about the legendary students of Oyama and knew what I had to do as uchi deshi, even if I die.

I got up, made a loud "Osu!" and dragged myself out to the middle and took up my last fighting stance against Kato.

There was a moment of surprise in his eyes and I saw a fleeting smile.

You...uchi deshi, sit down!- he commanded me with a thunderous voice. Just as well. I went back to the line alive!

He asked Ishi san to join him and spent the rest of the evening demonstrating technical points.

I remember it as the greatest night of my Kyokushinkai life.

But this is an aikido story.

I got a job soon after, moved out of Bondi Junction, graded two more belts and entered full contact competitions.
By December 1988 I knew very well that I would not make it far in the devastatingly brutal world of the Kyokushinkai.

One month later I enrolled at director Ken McLean's superb, Shin Sen Aikido Dojo at Paddington and found my calling.

I trained enthusiastically and graded for black belt after five years and I also got married, in 1996

My wife cared very little for aikido or master Ken. She found the whole notion of men running around wearing pleated pants,looking like skirts, ridiculous.

She on the other hand adored Patricia, the master's wife. We all did.

She was a tiny lady, a black belt and mother of seven children. Patricia was easy to talk to and she was always ready for a laugh. She also kept master Ken in check.

When on the mat, Tricia trained with real energy and if giant men became soft on her she was quick to point out she needed no special treatment.

In fact she was a motherly teacher to all of us. We were mostly young then (except for Harry who was around seventy!) with no children and we knew very little about family, responsibility, and how serious life can be.

I specifically enjoyed training with Tricia. She would often look at me and comment.
"You have so much power...now use that power for something positive " -she was such a great teacher.

We've had such a good time smashing each other into the mat!
Many fabulous years.

But then.

So suddenly...something happened. There was a change. Tricia disappeared from class and we heard that she was sick.

When you are around thirty years of age, you'd think you have all the time in the world.

When you have seven children you'd think that God will be gracious and look after you and at least will give you the gift of time.

But the ultimate foe, death appeared for her like a thick dark cloud in the form of cancer. Arrived ruthlessly fast too, giving her no time for a fair fight...and in the early hours of Wednesday April 8, 1998 Patricia was gone.

When I learned the terrible news my thoughts were.. oh no...not her. Not like this!

Did she at least have enough time to say her goodbyes to the children??!!

Deafening silence ruled that week.

It was somber and quiet next Monday evening at the Paddington dojo. I looked at John, Nick and Cary.

As senior students, one of them would have to teach the class. I thought there is no way that Master Ken would be here.
But at that moment the dojo fell totally silent.

We could all see our teacher walking in. The uniform seemed large on him now as he, so suddenly, lost a lot of weight. We all lined up and he took up a sitting position in front of the aikido scroll.

It was only two days ago, on Saturday, that we attended the memorial at the Bronte Surf Life Saving Cub. There were photos of Tricia on the wall, celebrating her life.

Shin Sen Dojo Paddington 1995. Aiki Institute director Ken McLean seated in the centre.

Shihan John Taylor (on left) with head instructor Jim Phillips next to him at the dojo in Bondi Junction 1987.

Many attended and we all walked around watching as she smiled in pictures. Smiles that we, her husband and her children will never see…again.

Overheard others talking…death is not the end…she is now one with the universe…no one ever really dies…it sounded all very comforting. But…tell that to the seven children left behind without their mother.

Later that evening I sat on the balcony with my wife in Bondi, still thinking about Patricia.

I let out a sigh. The oldest girl is 21 and the youngest of the seven is four. The little one will miss her mum the most- I said.

My wife shook her head. I was 18 when my mom died, it's been 6 years since and the more time passes, the more I think about her. I think the oldest will miss Tricia the most.

One day when her own daughter will be born, her first thought will be that mum is not here to see her- she added.

The little one will be looked after by the next woman who will come along in their lives…Hope there will be someone -my wife contemplated with misty eyes.

I didn't say anything, I was just happy my mother was still alive and lived just down the road.

This all went through my mind like a flash Monday night sitting in line I don't know how master Ken got the strength to come and teach. Tonight as we bowed in towards the scroll, he was Kyokushinkai, the strongest person I have ever known.

I had no idea that seven months later I would leave him and Shin Sen Dojo forever, after having trained there for 10 years. I would not learn the fate of the seven children.

It would take 23 years before I'd step on the tatami to train with grandmaster Ken again.

PS: As for you Patricia, up in the heavens, I still think of you and now I know, a kind woman did come along and saved your children. She saved them all.

Waiting at the door of the Kyokushinkai HQ Bondi Junction 1987.

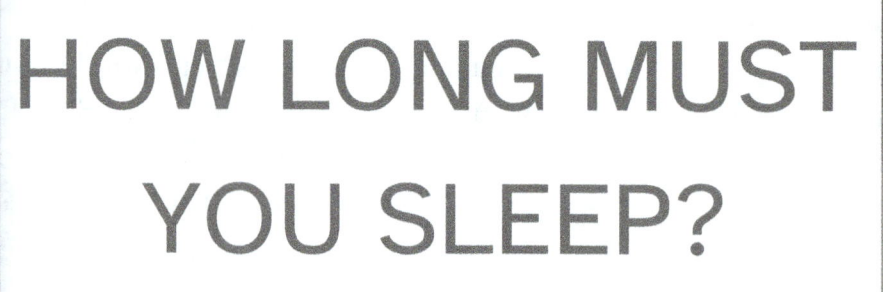

HOW LONG MUST YOU SLEEP?

by Mike Clarke

> "War is sweet to those who have no experience of it, but the experienced man trembles exceedingly in his heart at its approach."
>
> Pindar of Thebes

Two and a half centuries ago, the Greek poet, Pindar, knew a thing or two about violence. He lived in a world many today would consider extremely turbulent. Wars raged around and within his homeland, as city states and rival empires fought to gain control of more and more resources. You could be forgiven for believing such things are long gone, that human beings have progressed significantly in the last two and a half centuries, but you would be wrong. The world is no less violent and war torn now than it was back then. Humans just got better at destroying each other than they used to be.

In times past, you had to fight hand to hand or with unsophisticated weapons to kill your enemy, but that soon changed with the invention of slingshots, spears, and bows and arrows. Hurtling a projectile at someone from a distance made it conceivable for the weak to overcome the strong, and for the first time in the history of personal combat, it became possible to kill or maim without making physical contact. As humans grew smarter, their increased ingenuity was employed. Prime among them was how to make better weapons. The Chinese are said to have invented gunpowder, and from that invention sprang the 'next level' method of killing from a distance: the explosion. A method still in use to this day.

Strange then, that you and I, that is, we karateka, invest so much of our time and energy rehearsing ways to kill and maim people the old fashioned way, with our bare hands. Except that's not quite true is it? Many of you would no doubt tut-tut and shake your head at the thought of injuring someone to the point of murdering them. And yet you happily teach techniques that are, or so they are sold, meant to do just that, maim and kill. Even though you have no intention of using the techniques as they were intended, because you either lack the skill, fear the legal consequences, or both, you continue to sell them to others as something useful even when you know they are not.

Six or Twelve?
When challenged, the karate based self-defence expert will often quote; 'It's better to be judged by twelve than carried by six'. What an utterly stupid mantra that is. The logic of an adolescent mind yet to be tempered by experience and matured by years of authentic training. If you have never had a fight that left your opponent so damaged you found yourself standing before a judge, then perhaps the brutal nature of your fighting skill is not all you imagine it to be. Likewise, if the injuries your opponent received at your hands, and feet, are not so bad as to warrant you a lengthy time behind bars,

then again, perhaps a second, or even a third, look at just how effective your fighting skills are may be in order. Because for you, when it comes to a fight, it's probably best to have the names of six friends handy.

But wait, karate is about 'not' fighting, right? It is about developing your character. This is the 'do' you stick on the end of the word karate sometimes to give it an air of respectability. It also lends a level of defence to the argument used by a great many karateka, that you don't fight because your karate skills are too deadly to be used except in the most extreme of circumstances. Circumstances, I might add, that you never, in your entire lifetime, are likely to find yourself. Having just written that I can already hear the thousands of "but what if's ?" bubbling into the atmosphere from readers the world over. Look, I'm not trying to upset anyone here, I'm just trying to inject a little realism into this thing we all do. Karate speaks of having an empty hand, not an empty brain.

Becoming such as you are
Pindar also wrote… "Become such as you are having learned what that is." In other words, strive to be your authentic self. Although never an easy task, being an authentic karateka is made all the more difficult these days due to the shift in society that encourages the acquisition of fame over the attainment of skills and places the power of notoriety above the simple act of training. These changes began innocently enough, the quick dash to the side to grab your camera while the visiting instructor was demonstrating. Then came the mobile phones and tablets that could capture movement and sound, then the selfie, the YouTube channel, Instagram, and TikTok. So many today are more attached to their image as a karateka than they are to the training itself. I wonder, when was the last time you went along to a karate gathering and just trained? No camera, no phone or tablet, just you, in the moment, experiencing what you're doing and your mind committing that experience to memory.

If karate "isn't what it used to be," then look no further than yourself to see why that's the case. Then ask yourself…what have you turned karate into? When instructors say things like, "if I teach my students the same way I was taught, I'd have no students." I have to wonder, was that because the training was so poor it subsequently proved to be useless? Or perhaps it was so difficult only a few survived to reach a standard that was of any benefit. I suspect neither is true, and the march of time has simply altered the parameters of what is acceptable when using the word 'karate.' In reality, if you want to live off of your karate then you need as many people as you can get to give you money, and that means making karate all things to all people; easy, fun, exciting, family friendly, the list goes on. Rarely however, are new students taught to make their karate personal.

The real thing, or the great pretender?
Your karate is, like your life, what you make of it. What that looks like depends on you and how you choose to be in the world. You can be the person who blames everyone else for their misfortune, or the one who takes ownership of their circumstances, whatever they may be, and moves toward a better situation. You can become an example of the real thing, or a great pretender. If there is a 'path' involved in the learning of karate, then this is it. This is the personal 'journey' you hear karateka always banging on about. Knowing the destination you're trying to reach is important here, as your destination dictates the challenges you'll face along the way, and believe me, no matter what you are looking to get from karate, there will be challenges, physical, mental, and moral.

Returning for a moment to the idea that karate is a deadly unarmed fighting method that can kill with a single blow, perhaps a look back to the closing months of the second world war may prove enlightening. What follows is a partial translation of a post from a Japanese language blog called 'From the island of the rumbling sea'. The post was translated by my friend Mario McKenna. Mario has studied karate and kobudo for decades, was a long-time resident in Japan, and speaks, reads, and writes Japanese fluently. He is an avid researcher in karate history, an author, and an all-round good guy with absolutely no axe to grind. The original blog post in Japanese was about the Nakano Spy School, and how karate was integrated into the school's training. For ease of reading and to keep this article flowing I have, with his blessing, altered Mario's original translation slightly. A warning here, you may find some of the details that follow upsetting to read…..

The Aburayama Incident
In the book "The Truth About The Nakano School" by Sato Mitsunori, he discusses the 'Aburayama Incident' in which eight American POW's were executed at Aburayama in Fukuoka City on August 10th, 1945. Army officers ordered five of the eight POW's beheaded with a Japanese sword. However, two of the remaining three were to be executed with karate. This was done in order to test the 'effectiveness' of the karate techniques the officers were training in at the time. But the 'empty hand' executions did not go according to plan and all three were eventually beheaded with swords. The purpose of the karate training at the school was to attack U.S. troops. Dressed as civilians, the officers hoped to assist any rearguard action once the Americans had landed in mainland Japan.

The book includes the testimony of 'Mr. S', who participated in the karate executions. Mr. S was a graduate of the Nakano School and was assigned to the Western District Headquarters. On the day of the executions, he and the POWs rode to Aburayama in the back of a military truck. The eight POW were all Caucasian, and when they arrived at the execution site a hole had already been dug. The executions began in the morning and lasted until around noon. The prisoners sat in front of the pit, their hands tied behind their backs, none were blindfolded. As well as karate, bows and arrows were also tested for effectiveness, but it soon became apparent that neither of these methods was going to work.

The POWs must have mentally prepared themselves for what lay ahead because they were quiet and did not resist. The prisoner Mr. S executed was an officer… "he stared at me just before he was executed. I'll never forget that look. I began with karate, but he didn't die easily. After the first blow he closed his eyes. I was in a hurry and struck another two or three blows to the chest of the prisoner. When that didn't work, I kicked him down into the hole and stabbed him in the throat with my sword. I was so absorbed in what I was doing that I didn't think about the manner of the execution at all. I just wanted to finish it as soon as possible."

In the event of a battle on the Japanese mainland, Mr. S would have been part of a major force hidden among the local population, ready to fight a guerrilla war. He would be expected to attack American soldiers with karate, a tactic consistent with the 'Kokumin Kousen Hikkei' – 'Essentials for National Resistance'.

Recalling further his part in the executions, Mr. S said… "When I was in Nakano, we were trained in guerrilla warfare and practiced how to kill someone through execution. Even though we were ordered to do so, I have to admit that when I stood there my legs were trembling, and the handle of my sword was slippery with sweat, as was my forehead. At the time of the executions, I was like a robot following orders, and when I finished, I did not see the prisoners as human beings, but as objects. But when I saw the blood spurting from their necks, my eyes went blank. I had killed one of them. I can still feel it in my hands…" (page 102).

War Tribunal in Yokohama

Mr. S was arrested in December 1947 in his hometown where he was demobilised. He was sent to Sugamo Prison and was later sentenced to death by the War Tribunal in Yokohama. His sentence was however commuted to life in prison. That sentence too was later revised, and he was eventually released in August 1955. At his trial, former high ranking officers who ran the Spy School showed their ugliness (and cowardice) by constantly evading the court's questions, saying; "I don't remember giving the order", or "I didn't know." The U.S. military judges took a dislike to the former commanders who were now evading their responsibilities, commenting (page 106)… 'this reminds us of the words and deeds of the former commanders of the "group suicide" in the Karama Islands."

As a result of the orders issued by his commanders, Mr. S spent more than seven years in prison as a war criminal and lived the postwar period with deep psychological scars.

The stupidity of war, on any level
The Aburayama Incident took place shortly after the atomic bombs were dropped on Hiroshima and Nagasaki. At the same time as the United States was using the best of science to develop the worst weapons of destruction, in Japan, the 'Kokumin Kousen Nippaku' – 'National Defence Essentials', was being issued and farming and carpentry tools were being tested as weapons to see if they could kill American soldiers. What the U.S. and Japan were doing may seem to be at two opposite extremes, nevertheless both countries were engaging in the cruelty, stupidity, and madness of war.'

On Reflection
I think the moment of horror described here points to several truths that require mature and considered reflection. But one thing is certain, the techniques of karate are no more deadly than any other bare fisted fighting method, for it takes more than knowledge of punching and kicking to make real the myth of 'ikken-hissatsu' – 'one hit one kill' so often lorded as proof of karate's lethality. In truth, if you don't give yourself permission to kill, or die, when you fight, then you're simply beating someone up or taking a kicking from which you will recover. The modern day sanctioned brutality of the cage or ring, however vicious these fights may be, are wrapped in rules and safety. Neither of which will stop you from taking a beating but they will, in all but the most rare of occasions, stop you from being killed.

Finding yourself
Remember Pindar's advice, "Become such as you are having learned what that is."? Well, it's advice you will need to take on board if you aspire to be an authentic karateka. But first, you'll have to decide what 'you are'. Are you the instructor who teaches self-defence with only opinions to go on and no experience? Or the guru who fosters a need in your followers rather than provide a worthwhile example for them to take forward into their own life? Are you the icon, the influencer, the YouTuber? The seminar entertainer travelling the world divulging karate's 'secrets' to anyone willing to pay (and sneak off to the side to grab their phone to get a photo)? Or are you the karateka standing in your dojo, backyard, or kitchen, thinking about the problems your karate has put before you? Are you the karateka who turns up for training week after week, year after year, unknown other than by those who train beside you? Before you can 'become such as you are' you first have to learn 'what that is'.

You may well possess the physical skills to be an instructor, but do you have the mind and quiet courage to be a student? The way you pursue karate, not words, reveals the truth of who you are…it's blisteringly simple and utterly obvious.

Wake up to your dreams

So, how long must you sleep? How long must you dream of mastery while doing little to bring you to the place where you 'become such as you are'? A year, a decade? What a blessing if that were all it took rather than the lifetime so many give to their slumber. The fight karate addresses is real, and depending on your level of understanding, is aimed at either you or someone else. You decide who the opponent is and you decide how hard and how long to fight. You acknowledge your success and you struggle with your loss. Through such training you will, in time, come to appreciate 'what you are'.

And when you do, if you're not happy with what you find, then the choice is also yours; step back into the dojo and prepare to carry on fighting…or turn over and go back to sleep.

Books by Mike Clarke Available where all good books are sold.

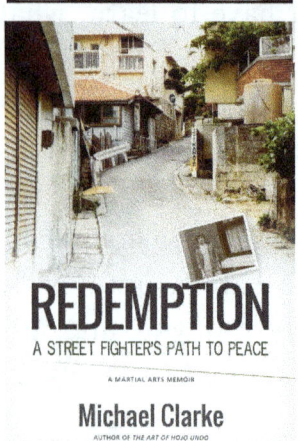

Real Kung Fu: Debunking the Myths of Kung Fu in China

by Ashley Couch

Master Bao

The global fascination with kung fu has led to an abundance of information—often riddled with myths and misconceptions—about the art form, its origins, and its place in the modern world. Online platforms like Reddit, Quora, Facebook, and Instagram teem with debates about the authenticity of modern kung fu, the impact of China's political history on traditional practices, and what truly defines "real" martial arts. Many of these discussions reflect a lack of understanding about the rich cultural heritage and the evolution of kung fu, shaped by centuries of history, adaptation, and a changing society.

As a full-time kung fu student at Maling Shaolin Kung Fu Academy training under a 32nd-generation Shaolin master in rural China, I have the privilege of living, practicing, and learning directly from the source.

This unique perspective, coupled with the guidance of my master and his kung fu brothers, has allowed me to access knowledge that is often difficult to find or properly understand online. In this article, I aim to clear up some of the common misconceptions surrounding modern and traditional kung fu, examining the realities of kung fu today, the effects of New China on its practice, and the question of authenticity when kung fu is taught outside of China.

Is modern kung fu 'real' kung fu?
Yes, modern kung fu is real kung fu—but kung fu might not be what you think it is.

The term 'gong fu' (pronounced 'kung fu' in the West) can be used in many fields as an achievement of perseverance, skill, and excellence within a field. It is a description of the level of a practitioner. For example, an expert in dance, opera, martial arts, hairdressing, cooking, acting, etc. can be said to have good 'gong fu' in their subject.

The term kung fu was introduced to the Western world by Bruce Lee. He used it to describe excellent martial artists, just as it would be used here in China. However, to the Western world, unfamiliar with Chinese language and culture, this adjective became a noun; a name for which they had only one association: Chinese martial arts.

So, if kung fu is a descriptive word for many things, what then, you may ask, are martial arts called in China? The answer: wushu. Wushu is the literal translation for martial arts and, despite the word's association (or rather, once again, mis-association) with 'modern' martial arts, it has been around for millennia.

The term wushu is used in China as the word for traditional martial arts, though, due to the spread of the web and media, they are familiar with the usage of kung fu in the Western sense. But, by traditional standards, a new or poor practitioner of Chinese martial arts cannot be said to be doing kung fu. Kung fu is achieved only through years of training, hard work, and dedication.

You may also be wondering how they differentiate, then, between 'traditional' martial arts and 'modern' martial arts (or what we in the West have dubbed wushu). There is no separate word for it. Wushu is wushu, and kung fu is excellence in wushu (and other categories). A school is known to focus on more traditional styles only by visitation, reputation, and a few other potential signifiers. Prospective students and parents may be able to tell from the name—traditional style schools may have the master or family name in the school's name. 'Modern' style schools typically have a much larger number of students while 'traditional' schools tend to be smaller.

However, the view within China of 'modern' martial arts is vastly different than that of the West. Where online forums and comments frequented by Westerners often perpetuate the idea that wushu (often specifically Shaolin) isn't 'real,' is diluted, is government-controlled, etc., Chinese practitioners, including Shaolin monks, think it has only improved. These varying ideals may come from different understandings of the purpose, evolution, and cultural impact of the arts. For the sake of simplicity, we will specifically discuss Shaolin going forward.

In the West, Shaolin is often viewed in a romanticised or archaic light. The general public tends to think of epic battles, meditation under waterfalls, mountain-top temples, superhuman strength, or even mystical abilities. It can be incorrectly viewed as a static link to a bygone era. This doesn't necessarily apply only to foreigners. In China, starry-eyed youths and those far removed from the influence of wushu also sometimes have a warped view of Shaolin based on movies, legends, and media.

Maling front gate.

Practitioners, and much of the general public in China, typically view martial arts, including Shaolin, in a few ways:

- A method of self-betterment, whether that be physical or spiritual;
- A functional form of self-defence;
- A sport.

Shaolin's original purpose has continually evolved over the centuries, from serving as a means to protect the temple and refugees during times of war, to a meditative and spiritual practice used to help oneself along the path to enlightenment, to a form of acrobatic enthrallment and physical transcendence.

It is seen to be ever-changing, adjusting itself to the needs of society and its devotees. After all, the rest of the world changes, why shouldn't Shaolin?

Now, how do Shaolin masters view the changes that have taken hold of much of the martial arts in China? First, I will introduce Master Bao, Buddhist name Shi Xing Jian, a 32nd-generation Shaolin warrior monk, under the esteemed lineage of Grandmaster Shi De Qian and Grandmaster Shi De Yang. Master Bao grew up training in the original Shaolin Temple and has dedicated his life to sharing the culture and excellence of Shaolin kung fu with the world. So, what are his thoughts on the matter?

I interviewed Master Bao for his valuable insight into the subject (and much of the content from the rest of this article). His perspective on the current state of kung fu offers a nuanced view of the ongoing debate about traditional versus modern martial arts.

When asked about 'modern' wushu, Master Bao's response was clear: it is excellent practice, and in some ways, it can be even more challenging than traditional wushu. The reason is that modern wushu incorporates visually striking elements—deeper stances, faster movements, and higher jumps—that demand greater physical agility, muscle power, and flexibility. These exaggerated movements, while sometimes criticised for their focus on aesthetic beauty, actually help practitioners build essential martial skills. According to Master Bao, if a student can perform these complex movements fluidly and swiftly, transitioning to traditional stances and techniques becomes more accessible and efficient.

In his experience, many martial artists who first train in modern wushu tend to excel when they later take up traditional styles. The exaggerated movements teach students to engage their whole body, making them more fluid and coordinated. Master Bao explains that in Shaolin, using the entire body for every movement is crucial. While one might perfect punches, kicks, or conditioning exercises, without this full-body engagement, the movements remain stiff and incomplete.

Master Bao observed that sometimes students understand how their body should move, but their body doesn't respond as expected. For this reason, in China, young students often start with modern wushu or a blend of modern and traditional. Modern styles and methods force them to develop the fluidity needed for martial arts. As they mature and continue their martial arts journey, they often find it easier to learn traditional forms because they've already trained their bodies to move with precision and grace. Those who begin with modern wushu and then transition to traditional wushu tend to be more adept than those who exclusively train in traditional forms from the start.

In essence, modern wushu serves as a stepping stone, teaching foundational body mechanics that are essential for mastering traditional forms and styles. While there's an ongoing debate abroad about the legitimacy of "modern kung fu," Master Bao believes that it is a valuable training tool—just as real and purposeful as traditional styles—and that the core principles of Shaolin martial arts remain very much alive and thriving today.

How did the rise of New China affect Shaolin kung fu?

Contrary to popular belief, the establishment of New China under the Communist government did not suppress Shaolin kung fu or Chinese martial arts. In fact, the government became a strong supporter of wushu and martial arts in general. After the founding of the People's Republic of China in 1949, national policies actively promoted wushu, even forming a national wushu team to showcase the country's martial prowess. All styles of Chinese martial arts, including Shaolin, benefited from this institutional support, which fostered both traditional and modern forms of martial practice.

In essence, modern wushu serves as a stepping stone, teaching foundational body mechanics that are essential for mastering traditional forms and styles. While there's an ongoing debate abroad about the legitimacy of "modern kung fu," Master Bao believes that it is a valuable training tool—just as real and purposeful as traditional styles—and that the core principles of Shaolin martial arts remain very much alive and thriving today.

However, a myth persists in some circles: that kung fu masters fled China due to political persecution and government attacks on their practices. This is simply untrue. The real reasons for the migration of martial arts masters were more complex and economic in nature. At the turn of the 20th century, China was going through major technological and societal shifts. The invention and rise of firearms—referred to as 'hot weapons'—diminished the need for martial arts in warfare. Where once a master skilled in techniques like the iron palm could overpower an enemy, no amount of hand-to-hand combat could compete with a bullet. As a result, the relevance of martial arts in combat began to decline, leading to a period where the art, while still respected, had less practical application.

By the early 1900s, during the collapse of the Qing Dynasty, China was rife with upheaval. Many martial masters faced economic challenges, not political ones. Without a need for their skills in the military or self-defence, some left the country seeking better opportunities abroad. This exodus was less about escaping government oppression and more about finding ways to support themselves and preserve their arts in an evolving world.

Master Bao

The Cultural Revolution (1966–1976), did bring a brief but significant period of turmoil for traditional practices, including martial arts. Originally supported by the country's leader (though, once its devastating effects were demonstrated he no longer favoured the reform), the Revolution was initially intended to speed up China's development by purging the country of outdated and harmful traditions. The government sought to create a new socialist culture, and young revolutionaries, known as the Red Guards, took radical measures to destroy anything they deemed part of the "old ways"—temples, shrines, historical architecture, and even traditional practices like kung fu were targeted.

The motivation behind these attacks wasn't anti-kung fu, specifically; it was a broader rejection of tradition in favour of progress. So, aside from the obvious economic reasons, why were so many youths against tradition and heritage?

Many saw old customs as dangerous and unscientific. In ancient times, if a child fell seriously ill, many families would turn to temples and pray for divine intervention rather than seeking medical care. These beliefs carried through the generations, creating a culture of superstitious neglect, ignorance, and rejection of modern, safe, life-saving practices. These outdated beliefs were seen as obstacles to modernising China and harmful to upcoming generations.

Master Bao in the Shaolin Temple

And so, revolutionaries sought to tear down the physical and cultural symbols of the past to force the country to move forward.

In this climate, traditional martial arts—including Shaolin—suffered. Kung fu masters, along with professionals from many other fields, were caught up in the sweeping antitradition fervour. Schools closed, temples were destroyed, and martial arts training went underground. The Shaolin Temple itself was largely abandoned, and many of its monks were scattered, though not permanently.

Despite this period of cultural destruction, martial arts in China endured. After the end of the Cultural Revolution in 1976, and particularly during the economic reforms of the 1980s, martial arts experienced a resurgence. The government again became a strong advocate of wushu, both modern and traditional, and encouraged its practice among the general populace. Shaolin kung fu, too, saw a revival. The rebuilding of the Shaolin Temple and the growing international interest in Chinese martial arts helped fuel this renaissance, leading to the global recognition Shaolin enjoys today.

Despite this period of cultural destruction, martial arts in China endured. After the end of the Cultural Revolution in 1976, and particularly during the economic reforms of the 1980s, martial arts experienced a resurgence. The government again became a strong advocate of washu, both modern and traditional, and encouraged its practice among the general populace. Shaolin kung fu, too, saw a revival. The rebuilding of the Shaolin Temple and the growing international interest in Chinese martial arts helped fuel this renaissance, leading to the global recognition Shaolin enjoys today.

It is important to understand that the persecution of traditional martial arts during the Cultural Revolution was not an intentional attack on kung fu specifically but a byproduct of broader anti-traditionalist sentiments. In the years since, the Chinese government has actively worked to preserve and promote Chinese martial arts as a vital part of its cultural heritage, allowing Shaolin and other arts to thrive once again.

Is Kung Fu Taught Outside of China Authentic?

What defines real martial arts? The essence of authentic kung fu isn't just a maker of technique, lineage, or style—it's a lifelong journey that requires years of dedication and practice. Real kung fu takes Time. The longer you practice, the closer you get to understanding the art's true nature, refining both body and mind.

With this prolonged effort comes the ability to push your body beyond its limits, and in doing so, your mind also begins to elevate, creating a balance between physical strength and mental clarity.

Kung fu is not merely external; it's an internal process too. As you gain strength, stamina, and flexibility, your mind sharpens. You start to perceive the world, and your place in it, with greater clarity. Over time, kung fu becomes a bridge, connecting your body to the universe. This connection between body and mind is what defines true kung fu mastery. It's not something you can achieve in a year, nor can it be taught by someone who has only studied for a brief time. Real kung fu requires years—decades even—of commitment and exploration.

Those who practice for only a short period and claim mastery are not authentic. There is no shortcut. To reach the highest levels of kung fu, both time and dedication are essential. Someone who practices for a few months or years and believes they are ready to teach is, in a way, deceiving themselves. Without a deep understanding of both the physical and mental aspects of the art, they are only grasping at the surface, while true kung fu remains far beyond their reach. This self-deception can be passed on to others, creating a cycle of superficial knowledge that lacks the substance of real mastery.

A true master shares not only their knowledge but also their lineage. Authenticity in kung fu is deeply tied to heritage. A master and their disciples are connected through an unbroken chain of knowledge passed down from teacher to student over generations. Kung fu, as we know it today, is the result of thousands of years of refinement. It is impossible for someone to create a new style or claim mastery without the guidance of a legitimate teacher.

Yet, lineage alone is not enough. Just because someone claims a specific lineage or dresses like a monk does not guarantee they are a true kung fu master. In some cases, people can even purchase lineage certificates without ever having trained with the master they claim to represent. Authentic masters must be able to demonstrate their skills, identify their students' weaknesses, and guide them to correct their forms—not just by saying, "That's wrong," but by helping them understand how to do it right. Real kung fu comes from relentless practice, whether it's repeating a movement a hundred times, a thousand times, or more. This is where true mastery lies.

Beware of those who claim their style is the only "real" martial art. This exclusivity often reveals insecurity rather than mastery. The more skilled a martial artist becomes, the more they understand that all martial arts share the same roots. While different styles may emphasize various techniques or philosophies, they are all interconnected. Think of the origin of martial arts as a reverse pyramid. At the base, all styles share a common source, and as you climb higher, you see how these styles have evolved and branched out. Then, the better you become, the closer you get to understanding that all styles, at their core, are the same, like an upright pyramid. If we were to visualise the full picture, this ultimately forms a diamond-like structure, going from knowledge of history: origins → styles, to understanding in practice: style → origin.

Some may think of styles like Tai Chi and Shaolin as opposites—Tai Chi being slow and gentle, while Shaolin is fast and powerful. But a true master sees the connection. It's possible to perform Shaolin movements with the softness of Tai Chi or Tai Chi movements with the power and speed of Shaolin. When someone has truly mastered a style, they can blend techniques seamlessly, recognising that the essence of martial arts transcends the boundaries of individual schools.

So, how can you tell if someone is a real kung fu master? It's not always easy. The ability to identify a true master comes only after witnessing many martial artists and developing an understanding of what real skill looks like. You'll know when you see it. A real master's movements radiate power, fluidity, and energy. Their agility and coordination leave an impression on those watching. For example, when Master Bao demonstrates during class, his movements convey intensity and power. You can feel the energy in the room as he guides students, showing them the difference between mediocrity and mastery. A true kung fu master is not there to please the student but to push them to their limits, ensuring they perform at their best.

Authenticity can also be found in a master's lineage. Their heritage and the way they teach provide clues to their legitimacy. But in modern times, many people seeking "real" masters are often looking for something psychological. Some enjoy the process of learning for its own sake. Others want to be pushed to their limits, seeking challenges that force them to grow. However, not everyone can handle the traditional, tough-love approach that is common in Chinese kung fu. Particularly for foreigners, the intense training methods of old may not be suitable.

In Chinese kung fu, the learning process is long and consists of several stages:

The Interest Stage: Everything feels exciting and new. This stage, which can last from months to a year, is filled with curiosity and enthusiasm for learning fresh techniques and movements.

The Bored Stage: After the initial excitement fades, the learning becomes more challenging. Students start to recognize the discomfort and difficulty in perfecting their movements. This stage can last 1–2 years, depending on the student. Some give up, defeated by the hardness of the training, while others press on.

The "Hang In There" Stage: Those who persist begin to find joy in the practice again. They start to identify their weaknesses and strive to improve. This is when they begin to grasp the essence of kung fu, though the length of this stage varies for each practitioner.

Master Bao's Lineage- Grandmasters Shi De Qian, Shi De Yang, and their master Abbot Shi Su Xi

Kung Fu Mastery: At this stage, a student can execute martial arts techniques with precision and power. They are in control of their movements and enjoy the process of training.

In the end, real kung fu can be found anywhere in the world, as long as the practitioner follows the traditional path of dedication, patience, and deep study. But there are no shortcuts. Real kung fu comes from within, built upon years of perseverance and practice, and guided by the wisdom of a true master.

Kung fu, both modern and traditional, is not a static relic of the past but a dynamic practice that continues to evolve with the times. What many perceive as the "dilution" of real kung fu is, in fact, a reflection of the art's adaptability and growth. From the support it received in New China to the new forms it has taken in modern wushu, kung fu remains a pillar of Chinese culture, rooted in centuries of wisdom, discipline, and spiritual significance.

Ultimately, real kung fu is not defined by outward appearances, technical jargon, or even geographical boundaries. It is found in the dedication, perseverance, and respect for lineage that a practitioner brings to their training, whether in China or beyond. As martial artists, we must challenge the superficial perceptions that dominate discussions online and seek a deeper understanding of the art's true essence. Whether modern or traditional, kung fu continues to thrive and inspire those willing to embrace its full journey—body, mind, and spirit.

MSKFA Student Photo

MSKFA Students Training

MSKFA students with Grandmaster Shi De Yang and Master Bao at the Shaolin Temple

Master Bao, 32nd Generation Shaolin Master
Translator: Lisa Guo, Academy Administrator
Author: Ashley Couch, Kung Fu Student
School: Maling Shaolin Kung Fu Academy China

Master Bao with kung fu hammer

Achieving mastery through kaizen is a beautiful Japanese philosophy that we should all practice and draw strength from.. in martial arts, business or in life, we should all continue to learn and have continuous improvements.

The kaizen philosophy has been applied around the world and used by business markets, martial arts, athletics and even in education .

Kaizen (改善): means continuous improvements, it comes from the Japanese words "kai" which means "change" and ("Zen") which means "good". It's a core concept in Japanese philosophy and business practices. This concept first gained prominence after World War II as a key principle in Japan's business rebuilding strategy, but its roots lie more ancient historic values.

What I love about the Kaizen philosophy is it teaches us that no matter what art you practice or what belt you are, there's always room for improvement. This idealism encourages all martial arts practitioners to constantly analyse their techniques, identify any weaknesses, and work towards self-mastery. As we navigate a constantly changing world, we need to learn that self-growth and improvement are ongoing processes.

Have you ever heard that saying "Martial arts is a way of life?" The same principles apply using Kaizen. As it teaches you how to continuously improve in your training regimes and your mindset. Which is a valuable lesson for all martial artists.

Remember, you're not just competing against an opponent; you're competing against yourself. The aim is not to prove you are better than everyone else. But for you to become a better version of yourself.

This is where the Kaizen concept takes centre stage. It encourages each practitioner to focus on making small incremental improvements. Maybe it's perfecting your stance, mastering a new technique, or even improving mental focus and endurance.

Think for a minute about something you have wanted to learn. Maybe you have even been teaching your kids a new life skill, and you broke it down into a step-by-step process. Making it easier to learn. That is essentially Kaizen!

- PLAN - let's say you wanted to learn a new kata or a new strategy in sparring. You can't simply say, "Let's do this!" You need a create a detailed plan, setting yourself achievable goals, a timeframe and obtaining advice from your sensei or coaches.

- DO - action phase. Now it's all about putting your plan into action. If you wanted to improve your kata, this is where you document every change you make to your stances, techniques, or focus. Get someone to film you before and after these adjustments and observe the outcome.

- CHECK - This is the analysis phase. Here, you take a deep look at the data you've collected. And compare your results against what expectations and objectives you wanted to achieve in the above phase. Did you achieve what you set out to do? If not, why?

- ACT - Finally, based on your analysis. Ask yourself was the adjustments you made successful. If so, take your training to a new level. If you were learning a new kata and you have now accomplished incredible stances and techniques. Now focus on adding your power and putting it all together. If it was not the desired result, then you go back to the drawing board, armed with this knowledge and insights you've gained. Then try and try again. Never giving up on the process.

By following this cycle of planning, doing, checking, and acting ensures that as a martial artist. You are always evolving, always improving, and never stagnating.

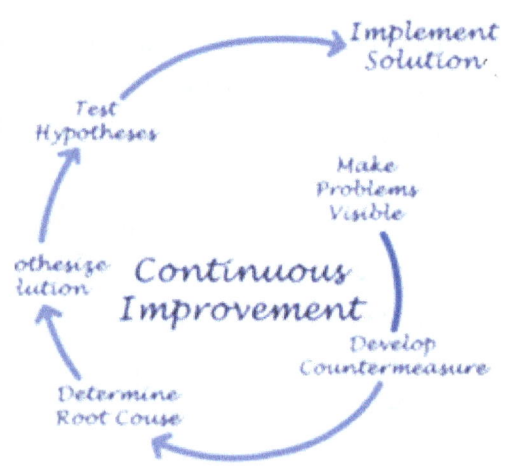

As you begin your martial arts journey, it seems almost impossible to master all the techniques that are required to earn your black belt and yet it is achievable if you take it one step at a time. There are no shortcuts. As you go through the ranks and with the guidance of your sensei. You will earn your black belt, just be patience with yourself and it will come. As we are living in a world that is constantly changing around us, our goals and objectives are in constant movement.

Martial artists are trained to have extraordinary focus, in particular in our technical skills and goals. When we progress up the ranks, our goal/target selections change and we must be mindful of this in order to achieve our long time objectives. Let's say you that you have done your new kata 50 times, you should always do it once more in order to improve. This is the power of achieving mastery through Kaizen.

Only doing the required amount of work in the dojo will only get you so far. But doing that one extra punch, kick or kata outside of the dojo is what makes the difference in your training and sets you apart. As this establishes the warrior spirit allowing you to achieve not only your goals today, but also in your future. You must always do more than needed to be a step above the other people as life is a competition.

It is your Sensei's job to give you the tools to achieve your black belt, but earning it is totally up to you. Only you decide if you want to train outside of the dojo. Some of the best training and character building traits are done when no one is watching you. It is up to you to attain greatness, to attain honour, to achieve that black belt. Kaizen is the path, and it is a path forged out of necessity and in a time where anything less meant death.

When you have your eyes set on a lifelong dream, it can seem both empowering but also a terrifying step to take. I'm sure nearly every one of us in our lives has gone through this same cycle. Start a goal, crash, fail, and repeat. At times like this, you almost want to give up, right? Luckily, it doesn't have to be this way. Instead, we can focus on making small, incremental improvements and lead the life we have only dreamed of.

We all know how hard it can be to start the process of personal growth, dragging yourself to training when it's freezing outside, or making those first adjustments to new techniques. It is important to get comfortable being uncomfortable.

Many people make New Year's resolutions like getting fit or quitting smoking. Everybody seems to have a rush of motivation. Yet, after a few weeks, it's all forgotten or they just don't have the time.

In the beginning, we want to make our first steps so easy that we can't make excuses. Always be kind and patient with yourself and allow your mind and body to adjust.

- If you want to go join the gym, start by just going once a week.
- If you want to be more active, take the stairs instead of the lift.
- If you want to write a new blog post, begin with a paragraph a day.

There's no need to overexert yourself. Take it easy until you feel comfortable. Once you have started a habit and it becomes a lot easier to be consistent in your efforts. You'll exceed your targets as you slowly build your momentum. It only takes a tiny push to lead you down the path of success. What is one small thing you can start today that you can't possibly skip?

At the start, your commitment and every small step builds on your foundation. Then, as you get better and you feel confident, you can go to the next level. Remember, if you're never trying to improve every day, then you will not improve and will stop growing. In karate, I have watched practitioners who have trained for years but stop improving. Not because they had no skill but because they only turned up physically, not mentally.

A martial artist who practices but never tries to improve on their weaknesses will remain doing their techniques wrong if they don't actively try to correct their techniques. Some improvements are better than no improvement.

You need to be fully focused on the task at hand. Ask yourself, how can I do this better next time? What minor adjustments could I make right now?

The purpose here is regular experimentation. What would happen if you used a different approach? Remember Thomas Edison when he invented the light bulb? He was unsuccessful on his first attempt. It took thousands of hits and misses. Every time it didn't work, he would re-evaluate his experiment until he found the right solution.

A common issue we struggle with is, we seem to have developed a mindset that failure is a weakness. Which is not the case at all, Kaizen shows us we need to choose the most balanced path. By pushing ourselves further when you see success. Accept failure and know it might not be the right time. Work out what you can do better next time and try again.

Taking small steps regularly in order to achieve your goals will lead to greater rewards. This is the magic of the compounding effect. Never unrealistically pressure yourself to be 50% better in a year. That's the exact pressure we are trying to avoid in the first place! Don't confuse results with growth. As we age and go through different phases of our lives, we then have a new set of small goals to set and to deal with. If your personal best is in your past, that doesn't mean you aren't growing.

Nobody grows in a straight line or exponential curve. You may have setbacks and plateaus along the way, but in the long run, it will trend upwards. If you focus on solving one small problem at a time. Love the process, not the results, and you may experience sudden breakthroughs as your underlying knowledge clicks together.

One thing I love about karate as that there is always something new to learn (a new technique or looking at something in a different context). This is why it's called a life long journey. The more you learn, the more you want to know.

Never fall into the trap of trying to reach perfection because it is unobtainable. Although this might sound terrifying, let it go and stay in the moment. Just think, if everything in your life was easy, and you had to put little or no effort into achieving something. Life would end up pretty boring because if there's no challenge, there's no real reward and therefore you stop growing.

Keep reevaluating how you are using Kaizen in your life. If you stay focused on something that serves no purpose to you. Why not let it go and use your time and energy that will reward you in the long run? Kaizen is not about impressing anyone else about how far you grown, it's about finding what pathway is right for you.

Nobody has complete control in their life when life throws you a curveball. You may think well, what can I do?

In Japanese, this kind of radical change is called kaikaku and can work in harmony with Kaizen. While somethings can be out of our hands, we can control our response. We are still the same person we always have been, even when circumstances come completely unexpectedly.

Kaizen plays an important part in how to react when a life has thrown you a curveball. We can lose focus when our lives become interrupted and unbalanced. But we should not be angry at ourselves if we struggle. We need to learn to be kind and patient with ourselves as we adjust. Everything will fall into place and it is okay to learn as your grow. You're human, after all.

Focus on yourself by asking small questions. How can I become more adaptable at this moment? Do I need to take a break to calm my mind so I can think more clearly? Remember, we do not have to take on everything on our own. It's okay to ask for help or guidance. Know in your heart you can deal with whatever life throws at you. Just take it one step at a time.

Kaizen is the practice of improving yourself or a process by taking small, incremental, daily actions, which then form habits that stick and, ultimately, makes you succeed. When you walk into the dojo, practice patience, awareness, positive attitude and work on making small improvements regularly; even if they appear slight because over time they will add up and be substantial.

This philosophy is an incredibly helpful skill to have in both our martial arts training and also our professional lives. Instead of trying to achieve everything at once. You should start with small, daily improvements. Just think, if you only focused on getting 1% better each day. Every little improvement you make, compound on the previous day's accomplishment. At first, the changes will seem inconsequential. Gradually, you'll notice improvements. Over time, you will be amazed at what you are truly capable of.

When is it Time to Hang Up Your Belt?
Navigating the Crossroads in Your Martial Arts Journey.
by Gary Johnston

For many practitioners, martial arts is not just a hobby—it's a way of life. The discipline, philosophy, and physical rigour of training become intrinsic parts of one's identity. However, there comes a time in every martial artist's life when they must confront a difficult question: Is it time to stop training? This pivotal moment can arise from various circumstances, each unique to the individual's journey. What might lead a dedicated martial artist to consider stepping away from active training?

The Physical Toll
One of the most common and valid reasons for considering retirement from martial arts is the physical impact on one's health. As we age, our bodies change, and the high-intensity training that once invigorated us may takes a toll. Years of rigorous training can lead to chronic injuries. Joint pain, particularly in the knees, hips, and shoulders, is a frequent complaint among long-term practitioners. Dr. Sarah Chen, a sports medicine specialist, explains, "Repetitive motions and high-impact techniques can accelerate wear and tear on joints. When pain becomes a constant companion rather than an occasional visitor, it's time to reassess your training regimen."

Some martial artists, like 45-year-old Brazilian Jiu-Jitsu black belt Mike Donovan, have found ways to adapt. "I've had to modify my training significantly due to recurring back issues," Donovan shares. "I focus more on technique and teaching now, which allows me to stay involved without exacerbating my injuries."

As we age, our bodies naturally lose some of their former capabilities. Decreased flexibility, slower reflexes, and reduced stamina can make it challenging to keep up with younger training partners or perform techniques that once came easily.

Master Yuki Tanaka, a 7th-degree black belt in Karate, offers a perspective on aging in martial arts: "The key is to listen to your body and adjust accordingly. At 65, I can't train the same way I did at 25, but I've found new depths in my practice through focusing on the subtle aspects of technique and mental discipline."

Another sign that it might be time to reconsider your training is when recovery between sessions becomes increasingly difficult. If you find that you're constantly sore, fatigued, or unable to perform daily activities because of your martial arts practice, it may be time to scale back or explore less physically demanding styles.

Life Pressures: The Balancing Act
While martial arts can be a lifelong journey, life itself often presents challenges that compete for our time and energy. These pressures can make consistent training difficult or even impossible.

Starting a family or even caring for aging parents can dramatically shift one's priorities and available time. Amanda Lee, a former competitive Taekwondo athlete, shares her experience: "After having my second child, I realised I couldn't dedicate the same amount of time to training without sacrificing my family life. I had to make a choice, and for me, family came first."

As careers progress, work responsibilities often increase, leaving less time and energy for intensive martial arts training. Long hours, frequent travel, or high-stress positions can make it challenging to maintain a regular training schedule.

John Mathers, a corporate lawyer and former Judo competitor, reflects on his decision to step back from training: "My career reached a point where 60-hour work weeks became the norm. I constantly missed classes and felt guilty. Eventually, I had to admit that I couldn't give my martial arts practice the attention it deserved."

The costs associated with martial arts training—gym fees, equipment, seminars, and competitions—can become a significant burden, especially during times of financial stress. While many find ways to continue training on a budget, others may need to prioritise financial stability over their martial arts practice.

Politics at the Club Level: When the Dojo Drama Outweighs the Benefits

Ideally, a martial arts school should be a place of growth, respect, and community. However, the reality is that human dynamics can sometimes turn the dojo into a hotbed of politics and conflict.

In some schools, issues of favouritism or power struggles between instructors or senior students can create a toxic environment. Sarah Kwon, a former Wing Chun practitioner, describes her experience: "What started as a passion became a source of stress. The constant politicking and jockeying for position within the school hierarchy took away from the joy of training. It felt like high school all over again."

Philosophical Differences

As practitioners grow and evolve, they may find that their personal philosophy no longer aligns with that of their school or style. This misalignment can lead to feelings of disconnection or frustration.

Master Carlos Gracie Jr., founder of Gracie Barra, emphasises the importance of finding the right fit: "Martial arts is not just about technique; it's about values and philosophy. If you find yourself constantly at odds with the teachings or culture of your school, it might be time to explore other options or take a break to reassess your goals."

In some unfortunate cases, practitioners may discover unethical practices within their school, such as financial impropriety, abuse of power, or a cult-like atmosphere. In these situations, leaving the school—and potentially the art altogether—may be the only ethical choice.

The Advanced Practitioner's Dilemma:
For those who have dedicated years or even decades to their art, a unique set of

challenges can arise, potentially leading to thoughts of retirement.

Experienced practitioners sometimes find themselves frustrated by a perceived lack of respect or understanding from newer students. This can manifest in various ways, from disregard for traditions to questioning techniques without proper context.

Advanced practitioners may reach a point where they feel they've plateaued in their personal development. The excitement of learning new techniques has faded, and the path forward seems unclear.

Brazilian Jiu-Jitsu world champion Marcus Almeida suggests, "When you feel you've hit a wall, it's time to redefine what growth means to you. Maybe it's no longer about learning new moves, but about perfecting the ones you know or exploring the mental aspects of the art."

The Impact of Stepping Away

The decision to stop training in martial arts is rarely just a physical one. For many, it involves a complex emotional and psychological process.

Many long-term practitioners find that martial arts have become a core part of their identity. The prospect of stepping away can trigger a profound sense of loss or identity crisis.

Dr. Lisa Feldman, a sports psychologist, explains, "For someone who has defined themselves as a martial artist for years or decades, the idea of no longer actively training can be deeply unsettling. It's important to recognise that your worth is not solely defined by your practice and to find ways to carry the principles of martial arts into other aspects of your life."

There's often a fear that stepping away from active training will lead to a rapid decline in hard-earned skills. While some loss of physical sharpness is inevitable without regular practice, many find that the core principles and muscle memory remain intact for years.

Some practitioners may feel a sense of guilt or failure when considering retirement, especially if they've made public commitments or hold teaching positions. It's crucial to reframe this perspective and recognise that evolving priorities or physical limitations are not a reflection of one's dedication or worth as a martial artist.

For those grappling with the decision to stop training, it's worth considering alternatives that allow for continued engagement with martial arts in modified forms.

Many practitioners find fulfillment in shifting their focus from personal training to teaching. This allows them to stay connected to their art while passing on their knowledge to the next generation.

Some martial artists transition to exploring the philosophical, historical, or strategic aspects of their art. This might involve writing, research, or lecturing on martial arts topics.

For those dealing with physical limitations, exploring complementary practices like Tai Chi, Qigong, or yoga can provide many of the benefits of martial arts training with less physical strain.

Rather than maintaining a rigorous daily or weekly training schedule, some practitioners opt for periodic intensive training sessions or attending seminars to stay connected to their art.

Making the Decision

Ultimately, the decision to stop training in martial arts is a deeply personal one. There's no universal right or wrong answer, and what works for one person may not be appropriate for another.

Grandmaster Jhoon Rhee, often called the "Father of American Taekwondo," offers this advice: "The true essence of martial arts lies not in the physical techniques, but in the principles they teach us about life. Whether you're actively training or not, a true martial artist carries these principles with them always."

For those struggling with this decision, it can be helpful to:
- Reflect honestly on your physical and emotional state
- Consult with trusted mentors, fellow practitioners, and healthcare professionals
- Consider your long-term goals and how martial arts fits into them
- Explore alternative ways to stay connected to martial arts
- Remember that stepping away doesn't have to be permanent

The Continuing Journey

The decision to stop active training in martial arts doesn't mark the end of one's martial arts journey—it's simply a transition to a new phase. The lessons learned, the discipline cultivated, and the friendships forged continue to enrich one's life long after the last bow in the dojo.

Whether you choose to continue training, take a temporary break, or move on to new adventures, the impact of martial arts on your life remains. As Bruce Lee famously said, "Martial arts is not about self-defence. It's about self-discovery." This process of self-discovery continues, on and off the mat, throughout our lives.

In the end, the most important thing is to approach this decision with the same mindfulness, respect, and courage that characterise the true martial artist. Whatever path you choose, carry the spirit of your training with you always.

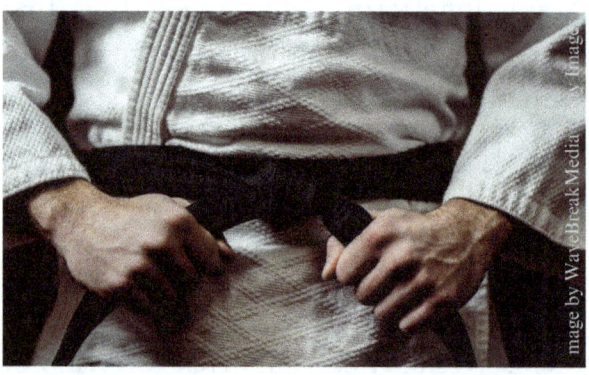

Teaching Yourself Hidden Techniques: Bunkai

by Benjamin Ward

"In the beginner's mind there are many possibilities, but in the expert's mind there are few." Shunryu Suzuki

Many martial arts styles harbour hidden techniques. One that immediately springs to mind is Gong Fu's art of Dim Mak, or deadly pressure points. The eight deadly strikes of Dim Mak are traditionally kept secret from the uninitiated or Westerners ("Gwailo"). Each technique is passed down through a tradition of Eastern philosophy, medicine, and martial arts, involving the use of energy and body points.

Eastern medicine offers concepts like the 'bubbling brook' on the sole of the foot. Massaging this point is believed to improve energy flow through your body, enhancing your connection with the ground, world, or universe. Similarly, Tai Chi concepts have often remained secret, partly due to cultural clashes and translation limitations. However, some instructors, documentaries, and even YouTube videos with Western presenters now explain these Tai Chi secrets.

One such concept is Zhan Zhuang, the basic stance of Tai Chi, which holds the central energy production and awareness of the art. It manipulates a microcosmic and macrocosmic orbit that we separate from at birth when our connected energy cycle with our mother is cut off.

Just as leaving the embryo is a key experience for all people, martial arts students often face a similar transition when they move on from their dojo at a certain age or level of experience. This transition allows them to experience life and their martial arts practice on their own terms, forming part of a martial artist's circle of life. Sometimes, this occurs when an instructor becomes too old to teach or passes away.

Achieving a black belt in most styles requires becoming your own teacher to a degree, putting yourself through training in your own time. Reaching black belt is merely the first step of the thousand-mile journey, one rarely taken every step of the way with guidance. As a way of life, everyone's journey will be independent and original.

This hidden knowledge within styles can be taught and learned from a place of not knowing it, similar to learning a previously unknown kata application. Some gradings are based on this concept. However, just as new approaches to other aspects of life emerge - like leaving home for school, going to a dance club, starting a new job, or attending an interview - each scenario involves showing up and using your aptitude to effectively deal with or enjoy the situation.

The concept of 'showing up' has been popularised in social media for gym workouts and by life coaches encouraging people to sit in the aridity or marinate in the unknown of a situation. This approach involves experimentation with unknown results. After contemplating how to organise your money, you might brainstorm an idea that allows you to stay within budget while still enjoying yourself. The key is to find a way to enjoy the process.

Self-directed training involves different levels of intensity and adherence to form. If you practice your fundamentals, routines, and rote learning, and still want to continue, you start to spend time where you've done all the prerequisites and can relax a little and just think about it. This leads to exploring areas you don't usually consider as important or have time for, potentially uncovering new techniques and training methods.

For instance, if you always train fighting techniques and sparring activities, and only practice self-defence in the dojo or with friends, you might find yourself standing alone, imagining an opponent or partner performing grabs or attacks, and visualising your response. This is a form of 'thought experiment', similar to a scientist contemplating a problem before building an actual experiment.

Martial artists can be like scientists, flower arrangers, or even renaissance figures like Bruce Lee, who explored various disciplines. They can also be like tradespeople, waking up early each morning and gradually building up to a fast and effective work pace.

Thought experiments in martial arts can occur when training self-defence, considering kata applications, or designing your own training sessions. They're unique in that they can be done in isolation or as a group, similar to the ancient Japanese practice of Koan meditation, where one contemplates seemingly unanswerable questions.

To explore this concept, try a game called 'Koan Crossing' with a friend. Find a quiet street with a zebra crossing. Starting on opposite sides, take turns creating and attempting to answer unanswerable questions as you progress across the road. This exercise encourages creative thinking and balance in martial arts practice.

Remember, you can practice these 'koans' or 'thought experiments' at any time, challenging yourself and others to find the best solutions. Your thoughts control your feelings, your feelings control your body, and your body controls your behaviour, which then leads back to the start of the thought cycle. Experimenting with this cycle can be both enlightening and enjoyable in your martial arts journey.

Koans are paradoxical riddles or stories used in Zen Buddhism to provoke "great doubt" and test a student's progress in Zen practice. They often appear irrational and are designed to help practitioners break through the limitations of logical thinking to achieve sudden enlightenment (satori).

Examples:
What is the sound of one hand clapping?
What was your original face before your parents were born?
Does a dog have Buddha-nature?
When both hands and feet are tied - how do you spring free?

Image by AnawatS - Getty Images

"The ultimate aim of martial arts is not having to use them." Miyamoto Musashi

The energy and enthusiasm of young martial artists training together, pushing their limits, and making their workouts uniquely their own is admirable. These 'bro-workouts', often occurring outside conventional gym hours, demonstrate how practitioners can personalise their training and find enjoyment in the grind.

This concept aligns with Vygotsky's early childhood theory of play, which he termed 'the infantile royal road to synthesis'. This theory emphasises the importance of setting rules as parameters, then expressing oneself within those boundaries to achieve the activity's aim.

In coaching theory, when students learn a new motor skill, they initially perform moves with stiff joints and limited range of motion. This is due to unfamiliarity and lack of conditioning. Through consistent practice, students experience a 'freeing' of their degrees of freedom. The instructor's role is to guide this journey with constructive criticism and encouragement, allowing students to develop naturally.

While there are various teaching strategies to enhance performance, positive reinforcement is crucial. Students must be given credit for their development, hence the importance of encouragement. One effective strategy is demonstrating new techniques (hidden from novices) correctly, even if performed by a senior student rather than the instructor.

Historical martial arts instruction often involved harsh treatment, as exemplified by the legendary Kung Fu instructor Pak Mei, 'the white-browed monk'. However, modern students are less likely to tolerate extreme training methods. While older practitioners may recount tales of tougher training, it's important to recognise that harsh treatment often stems from a misguided belief that the material being taught justifies such behaviour.

Eventually, students move on from their dojo, whether due to an instructor's retirement, relocation, or other factors. However, even while training under an instructor, the real work must be done by the student. This involves performing techniques with proper intent and emotional content - not anger, hurt, or joy, but a firm, unrelenting focus on progression and self-control.

When training alone, self-criticism can be both harsh and kind. It's beneficial to incorporate elements of gratitude, as seen in practices like Tai Chi. Acknowledging the universe as part of your training can provide optimism and a sense of purpose. Remember that your practice will eventually be shared with other students and instructors in your style.

Solitary training can lead to significant improvements in 'functional synergy' and 'unfreezing of degrees of freedom'. History provides many examples of self-taught artists and musicians who achieved greatness despite lack of formal instruction. The potential for martial arts expression always exists within your body, even if unrealised.

While it may be easier to learn a specific hidden technique, understanding the underlying principles of martial arts or the finer details of basic moves can be achieved through individual study. Embrace your journey, knowing that most steps will be taken on your own.

To bridge the gap between solo training and instructor-led sessions, try 'training with an imaginary friend'. Visualise your instructor or training partner, engage in imaginary dialogue, and 'hear' their advice. This strategy combines the benefits of solo training with the guidance typically received in a dojo setting.

Benjamin Ward's

The Fully Grown Grass Hopper

Essays on Martial Arts
Available
2025

Taking Care of Hamstrings

Hamstring injuries are a common problem for martial artists, especially those who take part in high-intensity training. These injuries can be debilitating and can take months to heal, so it's important to take preventative measures to avoid them.

First, it's important to understand what the hamstrings are and how they can be damaged. The hamstrings are a group of three muscles located at the back of the thigh that work together to flex and extend the leg. These muscles are responsible for movements such as running, jumping, and kicking. Hamstring injuries often occur when these muscles are stretched beyond their limit, causing small tears in the muscle fibres.

To prevent hamstring injuries, it's important to stretch and warm up properly before class. This can include a combination of dynamic and static stretching exercises. Dynamic stretching involves movements that are similar to those used in class, such as high kicks and leg swings. Static stretching involves holding a stretch for a period of time, such as the classic hamstring stretch where you reach for your toes while standing or seated on the ground.

In addition to stretching, warming up before class is crucial. This can include jogging, jumping jacks, or other light cardio exercises to increase blood flow and warm up the muscles. It's also important to gradually increase the intensity of your training over time to avoid sudden strain on the muscles.

Another way to prevent hamstring injuries is to make sure you are practicing proper form and technique. This means paying attention to your body and avoiding movements that cause pain or discomfort. It's also important to listen to your body and take breaks when necessary.

If you do experience a hamstring injury, it's important to seek treatment right away. Ignoring the injury or trying to push through the pain can lead to more serious damage and even longer recovery time.

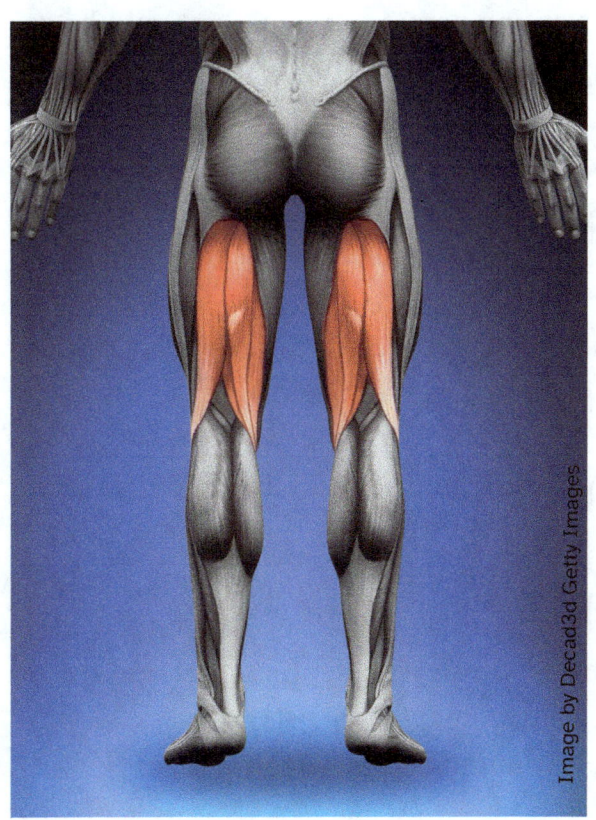

Image by Decad3d Getty Images

Treatment for a hamstring injury can include rest, ice, compression, and elevation (RICE). This means taking a break from training, applying ice to the affected area, using compression bandages to reduce swelling, and elevating the injured leg to reduce blood flow to the area.

Physical therapy can also be helpful in the recovery process. A trained professional can guide you through exercises to help strengthen the affected muscles and improve flexibility. They can also provide guidance on how to gradually return to training without further injuring the hamstring.

In severe cases, surgery may be needed to repair the damaged muscles. However, this is usually only necessary in cases where the injury is very severe or the muscle has completely torn.

Preventing hamstring injuries should be a top priority for martial artists. By taking proper precautions and seeking treatment

It's important to incorporate rest and recovery into your training routine. This means taking days off when needed and getting enough sleep and proper nutrition to aid in muscle recovery.

Hamstring injuries can be a frustrating setback for martial artists, but with proper stretching, warming up, technique, and rest, they can largely be prevented. By taking these preventative measures, martial artists can focus on their training and progress

Image by Gervin/Getty Images

Plus, Minus and Equal (PME) is a learning strategy popular with all kinds of leaders. Often attributed to UFC legend Frank Shamrock, the martial arts community has put it to use for decades.

The idea is not complex. In order to become great in your chosen pursuit, you require the assistance of three different people. The first is someone greater from whom you can learn.

Next is someone lesser you can teach. The final person is someone similar who can challenge you. These form the Plus, Minus and Equal. It's not surprising that this concept came from martial arts. Look at your own journey. We stand in line, ordered by grade and learning from the most experienced people in the room.

The structure lends itself to finding people who suit your PME system. As you continue to learn and develop, your position in the training landscape changes. Who are your Plus, Minus or Equal? It may be a single person or a group who fill each of these roles for you. These people are likely clearly defined.

Plus: The "Plus" is someone who is greater or more knowledgeable than you. These people guide your growth, and it is your responsibility to learn. In martial arts, the first person to fill this role is obvious; your instructor. The Japanese teaching title Sensei translates to "one who comes before." Your instructor is further along the same path, and they have already been in your current position. Whether you sought them out or were just lucky enough to stumble into their dojo, they have invested time into your learning. Your instructor even has their own Plus, a coach of their own, and is still growing and learning. Even very established coaches still find opportunities to learn.

"Every man I meet is my master in some point, and in that I learn of him" - Ralph Waldo Emerson. Your Sensei is not the only person who can fill this role. There are others with something to teach. More experienced or more talented, the place you train is filled with people who can show you how to improve. Consider the classes you attend: who has knowledge to share?

You might stand at the top of the line but some within your school are your superior in at least one aspect. Perhaps they have better footwork, faster kicks or can execute a kata with greater proficiency. Learn from them. The Plus can keep our ego in check. When we put ourselves beneath someone we trust, we accept that we have more to learn and that our education is not yet complete.

Minus: The "Minus" is someone who can learn from your experience. Helping others eventually leads many students into leadership. You don't have to be a master of a subject in order to have knowledge to share. Martial arts provide many opportunities for students of varying experience to assist in the growth

"When one teaches, two learn." - Robert Heinlein

When you undertake leadership, you become a more competent coach. Helping others fine-tunes your perspective. As you are forced to reflect on the strengths and weaknesses in your own technique, you will gain a greater understanding of yourself. It makes coaching exceptionally rewarding for both parties.

The Minus provides an opportunity to purge fear. Being the voice that leads others can be confronting. You are exposed to scrutiny and curious questioning. Confidence is a wonderful repellent of fear. Through coaching, the confidence of both sides rises simultaneously.

Equal: The "Equal" is there to push you to be the greatest version of yourself. They are a challenger or maybe even an antagonist. Early in your training, there are many who can serve as the Equal. Starting by comparing your progress to those with the same belt is ideal. You often find your Equal in competition. Striving to surpass them can inspire you to greater heights. Sport has produced many famous rivalries. Whether in the ring or the dojo, the Equal propels us forward by making us feel uncomfortable. For if the Equal continues to improve yet we do not, they are no longer our Equal. Eventually finding an Equal becomes more nuanced. The list gets shorter and not everyone at your level can fill this role. Many people form long lasting friendships through the Equal.

For now, you should identify someone with whom you regularly train as the Equal. Find reasons to challenge yourself against them, and seek inspiration from their achievements. "Show up, show up, show up, and after a while the muse shows up, too. If she doesn't show up invited, eventually she just shows up" - Isabel Allende

The Equal kills laziness. Their function is to keep you honest about your progress. If you do not keep up your education and development, it is very likely that the Equal will excel beyond you. Whilst it can be very humbling to lose an Equal, the flipside is the potential to gain a new Plus.

Getting the most from the PME strategy starts with seeking out the right people to fill each position. You may have read stories of immense success and people that did everything by themselves. These are lies. They are a selective telling of past events. It can be tempting to look back at our victories and decide that the credit is all ours. Whether we realize it or not, our success is built on the lessons we learn from others. It doesn't matter if these are learnt deliberately, by accident or perhaps by consequence, they still help to lay the foundation for our own work. Even writing this reflection borrowed extensively from existing pieces published by others. PME provides you with realistic and continuous feedback. It reveals what you know, what you don't know and the quality of your existing knowledge.

Over time your PME strategy adjusts. There is one constant: you must remain a student. Your belt can be black yet the learning is endless. Martial Arts teaches us to strive for perfection: an impossible destination. We are unlimited in our ability to get closer to it despite it always being out of reach. Dave Portnoy the President of media outlet Barstool Sports might be better known for his popular pizza reviews. Having tried hundreds of slices, he never gives out a perfect 10. He states that giving out a 10 would prevent him from going further, and that something better will inevitably come along. Martial arts and many other pursuits do not have a state of perfection. We are instead gifted with a lifetime of learning.

Kayne M. Dewhurst has been a martial arts practitioner since 1993. Kayne founded the Centre for Karate Excellence in 2006 and the previously popular OSMAT: Open Style Martial Arts Tournament in 2015. Holding a 6th Dan in Karate, he is also a Kickboxing Coach. Kayne splits his time between his hometown of Melbourne, Australia and Phnom Penh, Cambodia. Although he occasionally still teaches public classes for karate and MMA, Kayne primarily coaches school owners and professional fighters.

> "Perfection is not attainable, but if we chase perfection, we can catch excellence."
> Vince Lombardi.

Image by Artem Podrez

Respect in the Dojo:
The Cornerstone of Martial Arts Culture

by William Lynch

In the world of martial arts, few concepts are as fundamental and all-encompassing as respect. From the moment a student steps into the dojo, they are immersed in a culture that values honour, discipline, and mutual regard. This respect forms the bedrock upon which all martial arts training is built, shaping not only the physical techniques but also the character of those who practise them.

Yet, in today's fast-paced, often informal society, the nuances of dojo etiquette can sometimes be overlooked or misunderstood, especially by newcomers. As a result, even well-meaning students may inadvertently breach the unwritten codes of conduct that have been passed down through generations of martial artists.

In this article, we'll explore the multifaceted nature of respect within the dojo, examining how it manifests in various aspects of training and interpersonal relationships. We'll delve into why these traditions matter and how they contribute to a positive, productive training environment for all.

Respect for Instructors: The Lifeblood of Knowledge Transmission

At the heart of any martial arts school is the relationship between student and teacher. This bond, steeped in tradition, is built on a foundation of deep respect.

The sensei, or instructor, is not merely a coach or a fitness trainer. They are the custodian of knowledge, often representing a lineage that stretches back hundreds of years. Rachael Chen, a 4th Dan black belt in Aikido, explains, "When we bow to our sensei, we're not just showing respect to an individual. We're acknowledging the entire history and tradition of our art."

This respect manifests in several ways:

1. Attentiveness during instruction: When the sensei is speaking or demonstrating, all eyes and ears should be focused on them. Side conversations, no matter how quiet or brief, are disrespectful.

2. Proper forms of address: Using the appropriate title (Sensei, Sifu, Sabum, etc.) shows respect for the instructor's position and achievements.

3. Timely arrival: Arriving late disrupts the class and shows a lack of regard for the instructor's time and effort.

4. Appropriate questioning: While asking questions is generally encouraged, there's a time and place for it. Interrupting the sensei mid-explanation or challenging their teachings in front of the class is frowned upon.

One common misstep, especially among more experienced students, is the tendency to question or challenge the instructor's methods. While healthy discussion can be valuable, doing so in the middle of class or in a confrontational manner undermines the instructor's authority and disrupts the learning environment.

Mark Thompson, 3rd dan instructor at Southern Cross Karate in Brisbane, shares his perspective: "I always encourage my students to think critically and ask questions. But there's a right way to do it. Approaching me privately after class or during a break shows respect not just for me, but for your fellow students who are there to learn, not to witness a debate."

Respect for Fellow Students: Cultivating a Supportive Community

The dojo is more than just a training hall; it's a community. Respect between students is crucial for creating a supportive, positive environment where everyone can grow and learn.

One of the most important, yet often overlooked, aspects of dojo etiquette is the principle of non-interference. Unless explicitly asked, students should refrain from offering advice or correcting their peers.

Sarah Nguyen, a Brazilian Jiu-Jitsu brown belt from Melbourne, explains why this is so crucial: "Everyone's on their own journey. What works for you might not work for someone else. Plus, unsolicited advice can be really discouraging, especially for beginners. It's best to focus on your own training and let the instructors do the teaching."

Partner Work: A Delicate Dance of Trust
When engaging in partner drills or sparring, respect takes on a physical dimension. Here are some key points to remember:

1. Adhere to agreed-upon rules: Whether it's light contact sparring or a specific drill, stick to what's been established. Escalating intensity without consent is a serious breach of trust.

2. Be mindful of your partner's skill level: If you're more experienced, resist the urge to "show off" or dominate your partner. The goal is mutual growth, not one-upmanship.

3. Respect physical boundaries: Always ask before making any physical contact beyond what's necessary for the technique you're practising. This is especially important when demonstrating techniques that involve close contact.

4. Control your emotions: Martial arts training can be intense, but losing your temper with a training partner is never acceptable.

The Changing Room Conundrum

Respect for fellow students extends beyond the training floor. In many dojos, changing areas are shared spaces, and it's important to be considerate.

"We've had issues with people changing in the main dojo area instead of using the designated change rooms," says Emma Watson, owner of Warrior's Way Martial Arts in Adelaide. "It makes some students uncomfortable, and it's just not appropriate. Everyone needs to respect others' privacy and comfort."

Dojo Customs: Small Acts, Big Impact

Many aspects of dojo etiquette might seem like small details, but they contribute significantly to the overall atmosphere of respect and discipline.

The Significance of Shoes

The simple act of removing shoes before stepping onto the training area is loaded with meaning. It's not just about keeping the floor clean; it's a symbolic gesture of leaving the outside world behind and entering a sacred space of learning.

"I always tell new students that the moment they take off their shoes, they're transitioning into a different mindset," says David Chen, a Taekwondo master from Sydney. "It's about respect for the dojo as a place of focused training and personal growth."

Pitch In: The Importance of Helping Out

Setting up and packing away equipment might seem like mundane tasks, but participating in these activities is an important aspect of dojo culture.

"When students help with setting up or cleaning up, it shows they respect the dojo as a shared space," explains Lisa Brown, a Judo coach from Adelaide. "It's not just about lightening the load for the instructors; it's about taking ownership of your training environment and contributing to the community."

Gossiping and Complaints: The Silent Killers of Dojo Harmony

One of the most insidious forms of disrespect in the dojo is negative talk about instructors, other students, or the dojo itself. This kind of behaviour can quickly poison the atmosphere and erode the sense of community that is so vital to a healthy training environment.

"I've seen dojos torn apart by gossip and petty complaints," laments Michael Tran, a long-time Kung Fu practitioner from Hobart. "It's like high school all over again. But we're supposed to be here to grow beyond that kind of immaturity."

To maintain a respectful environment, students should:

1. Avoid speaking negatively about other students or instructors

2. Refrain from comparing instructors or styles in a way that belittles others

3. Address concerns directly with the instructor rather than complaining to peers

4. Focus on their own training rather than criticising others

The Deeper Meaning: Why Respect Matters in Martial Arts

While the specific customs and etiquette might vary between different martial arts styles and individual dojos, the underlying principle of respect remains constant. But why is it so emphasised in martial arts compared to other physical activities or sports?

Dr. Amanda Lee, a sports psychologist who specialises in martial arts, offers this insight: "Martial arts training isn't just about learning to fight or defend yourself. It's a vehicle for personal growth and character development. The emphasis on respect is a crucial part of this process."

By consistently practising respectful behaviour in the dojo, students develop habits that carry over into their everyday lives. They learn patience, humility, and consideration for others – qualities that are valuable in all aspects of life.

Beyond its role in character development, respect plays a crucial practical role in martial arts training. Many techniques taught in martial arts have the potential to cause serious harm if misused or performed carelessly.

"When you're learning potentially dangerous techniques, you need to be able to trust your training partners implicitly," explains James Wilson, a Krav Maga instructor from Canberra. "That trust is built on a foundation of mutual respect. Without it, safe and effective training would be impossible."

Preserving Tradition: Honouring the Legacy of Martial Arts

For many practitioners, showing respect in the dojo is a way of honouring the long history and tradition of their chosen art.

"When we bow, when we use formal titles, when we follow dojo etiquette – we're connecting ourselves to generations of martial artists who came before us," says Maria Costa, a 6th Dan black belt in Karate. "It's about being part of something bigger than ourselves."

As martial arts have spread globally, they've encountered a wide range of cultural norms and expectations. This can sometimes lead to misunderstandings or unintentional breaches of etiquette, especially in a multicultural society like Australia.

For example, in many Western contexts, a handshake is a sign of respect. However, in some traditional martial arts dojos, attempting to shake the instructor's hand might be seen as overly familiar or even disrespectful.

"I've had new students try to shake my hand after class," chuckles Sensei Tanaka, a Japanese-born Aikido instructor now teaching in Brisbane. "I appreciate the intent, but in our dojo, we bow. It's about maintaining the traditional forms of our art."

Another area where cultural differences can come into play is in attitudes towards physical contact, especially between men and women. While martial arts training necessarily involves close physical contact, it's important to be sensitive to individual comfort levels.

"In our dojo, we make it clear from day one that respect includes respecting personal boundaries," states Sarah Ahmed, who runs a women's self-defence program in Melbourne. "We encourage students to communicate openly if they're uncomfortable with any aspect of training, and we make sure everyone understands the importance of consent, even in a training context."

For martial arts instructors, cultivating an atmosphere of respect in the dojo is an ongoing process. Here are some strategies that experienced instructors use:

1. Lead by example: Students will mirror the behaviour they see from their instructors. Consistently demonstrating respectful behaviour sets the tone for the entire dojo.

2. Explain the 'why': Rather than simply enforcing rules, take the time to explain the reasoning behind dojo etiquette. Understanding the purpose behind these customs can increase buy-in from students.

3. Address breaches promptly: When disrespectful behaviour occurs, address it immediately but discreetly. Use it as a teaching opportunity rather than a punishment.

4. Recognise and reward respectful behaviour: Publicly acknowledging students who consistently demonstrate good dojo etiquette can reinforce its importance.

5. Incorporate etiquette into gradings: Make knowledge and practice of dojo etiquette a formal part of the grading process.

For new students, the myriad rules and customs of the dojo can sometimes feel overwhelming. It's important to remember that learning proper etiquette is a process, just like learning physical techniques.

"When I first started training, I was constantly worried about making etiquette mistakes," recalls Tom Baker, now a black belt in Judo. "But I realised that as long as I was making an honest effort and was open to correction, my seniors and instructors were patient with me. It's not about perfection; it's about sincere effort."

Some tips for students working to improve their dojo etiquette:

1. Observe senior students: Watch how more experienced practitioners behave and interact in the dojo.

2. Ask questions: If you're unsure about a point of etiquette, ask your instructor or a senior student. They'll appreciate your desire to learn and do things correctly.

3. Reflect on your training: After each session, take a moment to consider how you conducted yourself. Did you show proper respect to your instructor, training partners, and the dojo itself?

4. Be patient with yourself: Learning proper dojo etiquette takes time. Don't be too hard on yourself if you make mistakes; instead, focus on continuous improvement.

In the end, respect in the dojo is about more than just following a set of rules or adhering to tradition. It's about creating an environment where everyone can learn, grow, and challenge themselves safely and positively. It's about acknowledging the efforts of those who have gone before us and paving the way for those who will come after. It's about transforming not just our bodies, but our characters.

As martial artists, we have the opportunity to carry the principle of respect beyond the dojo walls and into our daily lives. In doing so, we not only honour the traditions of our chosen arts but also contribute to creating a more respectful, harmonious society.

In the words of Jigoro Kano, the founder of Judo:

"The ultimate objective of Judo discipline is to be utilised as a means to progress along the road to self-perfection, and thence to contribute something of value to the world."

By cultivating deep respect - for our instructors, our fellow students, our art, and ourselves - we take important steps along that road.

Whether you're a seasoned black belt or a beginner just stepping onto the mats for the first time, remember that every bow, every "Osu," every moment of focused attention is an opportunity to embody the core values of martial arts. In a world that often seems to be losing touch with the importance of respect, the dojo stands as a beacon - a place where mutual respect isn't just encouraged, but essential.

The next time you step into the dojo, take a moment to reflect on the deeper meaning behind the rituals and etiquette. In that simple act of removing your shoes, in the crisp snap of your gi as you bow, in the focused silence as your sensei demonstrates a technique, you're not just practising moves - you're participating in a centuries-old tradition of respect, discipline, and continuous self-improvement.

And that, perhaps, is the greatest respect of all - respect for the transformative power of martial arts themselves.

Image by Mashabubba, Getty Images

Raising the Bar in Coaching: Leveraging the Power of Focused Drills for long term student development

As karate instructors, the challenge is to keep classes both engaging and effective. We've all heard variations of 'something old, something new and something interesting to do' and while it's essential to master specific techniques, avoiding repetitive routines is key to sustaining long-term interest and growth. By refining our approach and targeting various aspects of karate through focused drills, we can help our students build a well-rounded skill set.

Keeping Training Dynamic: The Role of Varied Drills

Variety is crucial in keeping karate training fresh and effective. Rather than simply running through katas, a simple approach for new instructors could be to break them down into their essential components. This approach allows students to deepen their understanding and execution of each movement, ultimately leading to mastery of complex techniques.

For instance, focusing on the finer points of stances, timing, or breath control during a session can significantly enhance a student's overall performance when these elements are later pieced together in kata practice.

The Benefits of a Daily Training Intent

Begin each class with a clear "focus of the class" that targets a specific aspect of your karate technique. For example, if the focus is on breath work, drills might include:

1. Breath Control Exercises - Practising deep, controlled breathing to maintain calmness and focus.

2. Timing Drills - Coordinating breath with movement to maximise efficiency and power.

3. Kata Application - Integrating breath control and timing within a specific kata sequence.

Breath work is often an underappreciated aspect of karate, yet it is vital for maintaining endurance, focus, and effective technique. By concentrating on breathing and timing, students can develop a deeper sense of connection and whilst the drill may be focused on kata in a particular class, the drill format can be applied to kumite or other basic drills.

This approach also ensures that each training session can build on the last, allowing students to internalise key components before progressing to more complex applications.

Learning Through Experimentation and Adaptation

New instructors might find it challenging to structure classes around a specific focus, but this practice is crucial for both personal growth and student development. As you explore different aspects of karate, you'll uncover nuances in techniques that deepen your understanding.

Experimentation is also essential. Trying new drills, even if some don't work as expected, leads to valuable insights and adaptations that can benefit your students. Trust in your experience, and don't be afraid to innovate.

Conclusion: Embracing Focus and Variety in Karate Training

As you plan your training cycles, remember that combining variety with a focused approach is essential to keeping karate training dynamic and effective. By introducing different drills and honing in on specific performance aspects, you'll maintain student engagement and help them achieve their full potential. Continue to learn, adapt, and innovate, guiding your students to new heights in their karate journey.

Author Bio:

Paul Pirie is a 5th Dan Kimura Shukokai Karate and started his karate journey under Shihan Chris Thompson (9th Dan) in South Africa. Paul and his dojo are active members of Kimura Shukokai International (KSI) and he travels overseas at least once a year to train and learn. Paul has been teaching karate since 1996 and founded Samurai Dojo Australia – Kimura Shukokai Karate in 2014.

Email: hello@samuraidojo.com.au
Website: www.samuraidojo.com.au
Instagram: https://www.instagram.com/samurai_dojo_aus/
Facebook: https://www.facebook.com/SamuraiDojoAustralia

Image by Ryan McVay

In the world of martial arts, we often focus on high-intensity training, complex techniques, and rigorous conditioning. But what if one of the most powerful tools for improving your martial arts practice was something as simple and accessible as walking? It might sound too good to be true, but the humble act of putting one foot in front of the other could be the secret weapon you've been overlooking in your quest for martial arts mastery.

The Unexpected Connection

At first glance, walking might seem far removed from the dynamic movements of martial arts. After all, how could a leisurely stroll compare to the intensity of a sparring session or the precision of kata practice? But dig a little deeper, and you'll find that walking and martial arts share more common ground than you might think.

Walking is the foundation of human movement, it involves balance, coordination, and a constant shift of weight from one leg to the other. These are all fundamental principles in martial arts as well.

Many martial arts techniques, from the basic horse stance in kung fu to the fluid footwork of boxing, have their roots in the simple act of walking. By honing this fundamental movement, we lay the groundwork for more complex techniques.

Physical Benefits: Building the Foundation

Let's start with the obvious: the physical benefits of walking. While it might not be as flashy as a spinning kick or as intense as a heavy bag workout, walking offers a range of physical benefits that can directly translate to improved martial arts performance.

1. Endurance and Stamina

One of the most significant benefits of regular walking is improved cardiovascular endurance. Many people underestimate the cardiovascular benefits of walking. A brisk 30-minute walk can significantly improve your heart health and lung capacity.

This increased endurance can translate directly to your martial arts practice. Whether you're engaged in a lengthy sparring session or performing a complex kata, having a strong cardiovascular base allows you to maintain your performance for longer periods without fatigue.

2. Lower Body Strength and Stability

Walking, especially on varied terrain or uphill, can help strengthen the muscles in your legs and feet. This increased lower body strength and stability is crucial in martial arts, where a solid foundation is key to generating power and maintaining balance.

"I noticed a significant improvement in my stances after I started incorporating regular walks into my routine," shares

Lisa Nguyen, a Wing Chun practitioner from Perth. "My horse stance became more stable, and my footwork in chi sau (sticky hands) drills improved noticeably."

3. Joint Health and Flexibility

Unlike high-impact activities, walking is gentle on your joints while still providing enough stimulus to keep them healthy and mobile. This is particularly beneficial for martial artists, who often put significant stress on their joints during training.

Walking helps lubricate the joints and keeps them flexible. This can help prevent injuries and improve overall mobility, which is crucial in martial arts where flexibility and range of motion are so important.

4. Recovery and Active Rest

Walking can also serve as an excellent form of active recovery between intense training sessions. It promotes blood flow to muscles, helping to reduce soreness and speed up recovery without putting additional stress on the body.

Mental Benefits: Sharpening the Warrior Mind

While the physical benefits of walking are significant, it's perhaps the mental benefits that make it such a powerful tool for martial artists. After all, martial arts is as much a mental discipline as it is a physical one.

1. Stress Reduction and Mental Clarity

Walking, especially in nature, has been shown to reduce stress and improve mental clarity. This can be invaluable for martial artists, helping to clear the mind before training or competitions.

"I often go for a walk before a big tournament," says Jake Wilson, a judo competitor from Brisbane. "It helps me clear my head and focus on the task ahead. I find I perform much better when I've had that time to mentally prepare."

2. Mindfulness and Present-Moment Awareness

Walking provides an excellent opportunity to practice mindfulness, a skill that's crucial in martial arts. By focusing on the sensation of your feet hitting the ground, the rhythm of your breath, or the sights and sounds around you, you can develop a stronger sense of present-moment awareness.

"The mindfulness I practice during my daily walks has significantly improved my focus during training," shares Emma Taylor, a Tai Chi instructor from Adelaide. "I'm more aware of my body, my breathing, and my surroundings, which translates to better performance in my forms and push hands practice."

3. Problem-Solving and Creativity

Many people find that walking helps stimulate creative thinking and problem-solving. This can be particularly useful in martial arts, where creative solutions and adaptability are often key to success.

4. Emotional Regulation

Regular walking has been shown to help regulate emotions and improve mood. This emotional stability can be a significant asset in martial arts, where keeping a cool head under pressure is often crucial.

Here are some practical strategies to harness the power of walking to enhance your martial arts training.

1. Walking Meditation

Try incorporating walking meditation into your routine. This involves walking slowly and mindfully, focusing on the sensation of each step. This practice can help develop the mind-body connection that's so crucial in martial arts.

2. Nature Walks for Visualization

Use walks in nature as an opportunity for visualization practice. Imagine yourself performing techniques or kata perfectly, or visualize success in your next competition. The relaxed state induced by walking can make these visualizations particularly powerful.

3. Interval Walking for Endurance

To build endurance, try interval walking. Alternate periods of brisk walking with periods of slower walking. This mimics the rhythms of many martial arts competitions, where bursts of intense activity are interspersed with periods of relative calm.

4. Walking as Active Recovery

Incorporate gentle walks into your rest days as a form of active recovery. This can help reduce muscle soreness and keep you moving without overtaxing your body.

5. Pre-Training Walks

Consider going for a short walk before your martial arts training sessions. This can serve as a physical warm-up and a mental preparation, helping you transition from your daily life to your training mindset.

6. Mindful Cool-Down

After intense training sessions, a mindful walk can serve as an excellent cool-down, allowing your body to gradually return to its resting state while you reflect on your training.

Despite the benefits, some martial artists might be sceptical about incorporating walking into their training regimen. Let's address some common concerns:

"Walking isn't intense enough for martial artists."

While it's true that walking isn't as intense as many martial arts drills, it's not meant to replace your regular training. Instead, it complements it, providing a foundation of endurance, stability, and mental focus that can enhance your more intense training sessions.

"Walking is boring."

If you find walking boring, try making it more engaging. Listen to martial arts podcasts or audiobooks while you walk, use the time for visualisation practice, or invite a training partner to join you for walking discussions about techniques or strategy.

The Walking Warrior: A Holistic Approach

By integrating walking into your martial arts practice, you're adopting a more holistic approach to your training. You're not just developing your body, but also your mind and spirit - the three elements that form the core of true martial arts mastery.

> "The martial artist who neglects any aspect of their development - physical, mental, or spiritual - will always be limited," says Grandmaster Lee, "Walking offers a simple yet powerful way to develop all three aspects simultaneously."

Walking is a practice that can stay with you throughout your entire martial arts journey. While high-intensity training might become more challenging as you age, walking is a form of exercise that you can continue well into your later years, allowing you to maintain your connection to martial arts principles even when active training becomes difficult.

In the quest for martial arts excellence, it's easy to get caught up in the search for secret techniques or advanced training methods. But sometimes, the most powerful tools are the simplest ones. Walking - this most basic of human movements - offers a wealth of benefits that can enhance every aspect of your martial arts practice.

From building physical endurance and stability to fostering mental clarity and emotional balance, walking can be the secret weapon that takes your martial arts practice to the next level. It's accessible, adaptable, and can be integrated into your life and training in countless ways.

The next time you're looking for a way to enhance your martial arts journey, consider lacing up your shoes and heading out for a walk. With each step, you'll be building a stronger foundation for your practice, developing the body, mind, and spirit of a true martial artist.

Every journey, no matter how long or challenging, begins with a single step. Your journey to martial arts mastery is no different. So why not take that step today? The path of the walking warrior awaits.

Spring Vegetable & Chicken, Quinoa Power Bowl

Ingredients (Serves 2):
- 1 cup quinoa, rinsed
- 2 boneless, skinless chicken breasts
- 2 cups mixed spring vegetables)
- 1 cup cherry tomatoes, halved
- 1/4 cup crumbled feta cheese
- 2 tbsp olive oil
- 1 lemon, juiced
- 1 tsp dried oregano
- Salt and pepper to taste

Instructions:
1. Cook quinoa according to package instructions. Set aside.
2. Season chicken breasts with salt, pepper, and oregano.
3. Grill chicken for 6-7 minutes per side, or until cooked through. Let rest for five minutes, then slice.
4. Steam the asparagus and peas for 3-4 minutes until tender-crisp.
5. In a large bowl, combine cooked quinoa, steamed vegetables, and baby spinach.
6. Add cherry tomatoes and sliced chicken to the bowl.
7. Drizzle with olive oil and lemon juice, then toss to combine.
8. Top with crumbled feta cheese and serve.

Salmon and Spring Greens Salad with Citrus Dressing

Ingredients (Serves 2):
- 2 salmon fillets (about 150g each)
- 4 cups mixed spring greens
- 1 avocado, sliced
- 1/2 cup strawberries, sliced
- 1/4 cup walnuts, roughly chopped
- 2 tbsp pumpkin seeds

For the dressing:
- 2 tbsp olive oil
- 1 orange, juiced
- 1 tsp honey
- 1 tsp Dijon mustard
- Salt and pepper

Instructions:
1. Preheat the oven to 200°C (400°F).
2. Season salmon fillets with salt and pepper, then bake for 12-15 minutes until cooked through.
3. While the salmon is cooking, prepare the dressing by whisking together olive oil, orange juice, honey, Dijon mustard, salt, and pepper.
4. In a large bowl, toss the mixed spring greens with half of the dressing.
5. Divide the dressed greens between two plates.
6. Top each salad with sliced avocado, strawberries, walnuts, and pumpkin seeds.
7. Once the salmon is cooked, place a fillet on top of each salad.
8. Drizzle the remaining dressing over the salads and serve.

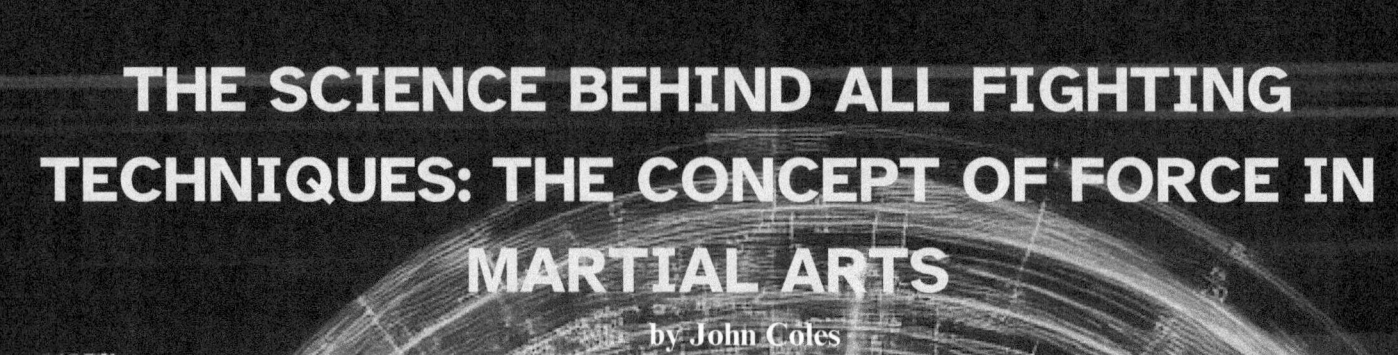

THE SCIENCE BEHIND ALL FIGHTING TECHNIQUES: THE CONCEPT OF FORCE IN MARTIAL ARTS

by John Coles

Image by Kempter, Getty Images

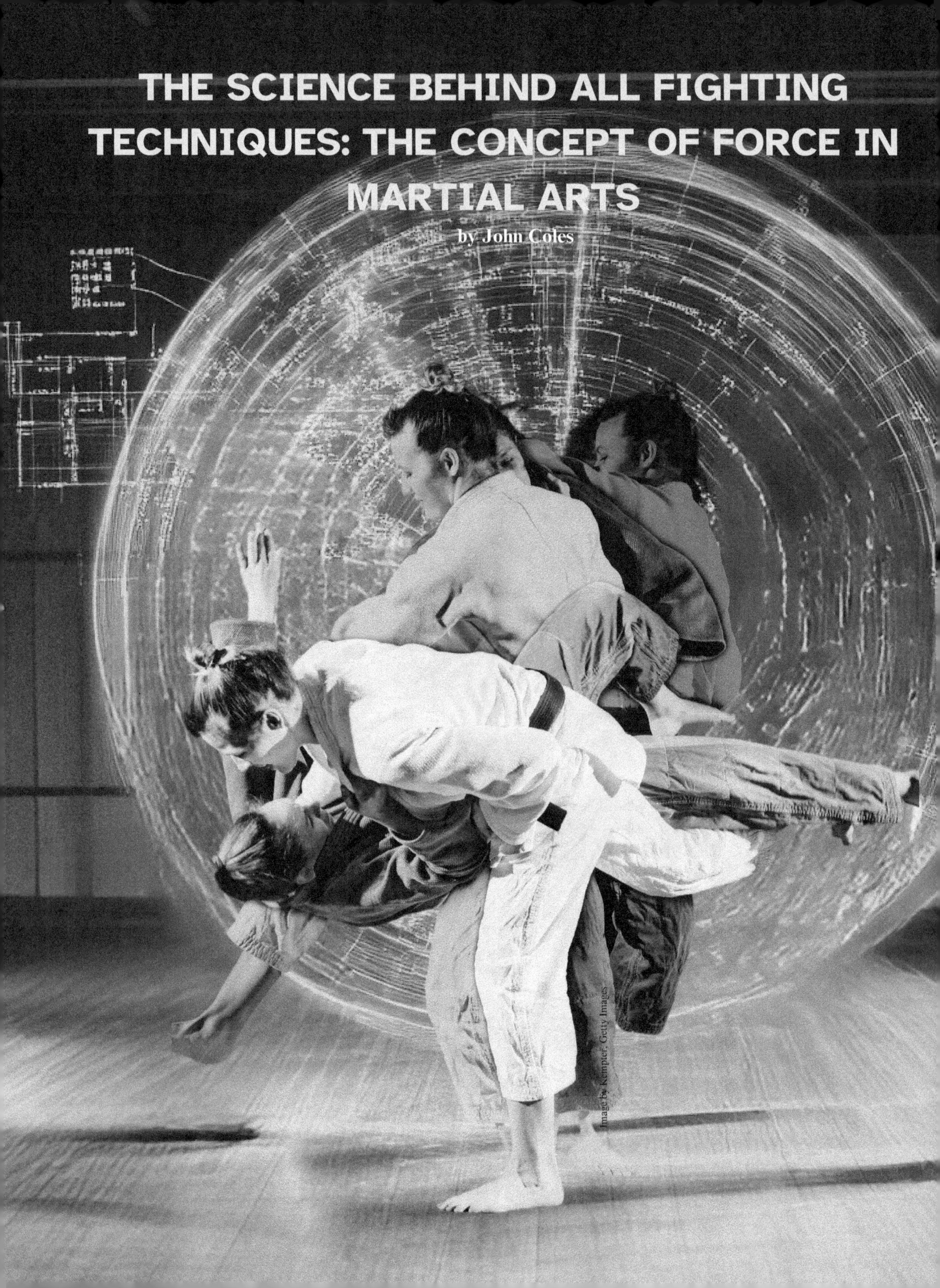

In martial arts, understanding how and why a technique works is as important as knowing how to perform it. In fact, a black belt shouldn't be just a marker of physical skill, but also an indication of deep theoretical knowledge. As Gracie and Gracie (2001) point out, a black belt understands the biomechanical principles behind every move (or at least they should), not just how to execute it. But what exactly does this mean?

What is Force?
The concept of force is central to the effectiveness of every martial arts technique. It's what causes the body to start, stop, change speed, or alter direction. It's also responsible for deforming tissue to cause pain or injury, depending on how much force is applied. In biomechanics, force is defined simply as a push or a pull that changes or changes the motion or shape of a body. These forces are what make martial arts techniques, self-defence, and combat training effective in real-world encounters.

Analysing Forces in Techniques
When analysing any martial arts technique, you can break it down into key components that focus on the forces involved:

Point of Application (PoA): Identify where the force is applied. For a throw, this might be the grip on your opponent's sleeve or lapel.

Type of Force: Determine whether the force is a push or a pull.

Direction: Assess the direction of the applied force (e.g., forward, upward, at an angle).

Magnitude: Consider how much force is applied, focusing on relative measures rather than specific numbers.

Objective: Understand the purpose of the force—whether it's to change the opponent's motion (e.g., to unbalance them) or to deform their tissue (e.g., joint locks that cause pain or injury).

By systematically examining these elements, practitioners can gain deeper insights into the mechanics of techniques and how to improve their effectiveness.

Kano and the Force of Unbalancing
The founder of Kodokan Judo, Jigoro Kano, offered a beautifully simple explanation of the force behind one of judo's most foundational concepts: kuzushi, or unbalancing. According to Kano (1986), unbalancing is done through pushing and pulling the opponent with the whole body, not just the arms. This concept captures the essence of applying forces in martial arts. Kano's description of kuzushi as pushing and pulling in eight directions (happo no kuzushi) exemplifies how a force-based understanding enhances technical mastery.

Practical Example: The Forces Behind Ogoshi

Take ogoshi (major hip throw) as an example. Kano (1986) breaks this throw into three stages: kuzushi (unbalancing), tsukuri (positioning), and kake (execution). Each stage involves distinct forces that interact to achieve the desired outcome. During kuzushi, for instance, the judoka applies a pulling force to break the opponent's balance forward or to the right front corner. In kake, the judoka's knees straighten, applying an upward pushing force that lifts the opponent off the ground while continuing to pull with the hands in a circular direction.

By analysing the forces at play in these phases, students can better understand how to generate the power needed to execute the throw and where they might be going wrong if the technique doesn't work. Teaching with a force-based approach helps students to visualise the mechanics and sharpen their execution.

Teaching with Forces: A New Paradigm

The key to mastering martial arts isn't just in physical repetition, but in understanding the forces involved in each movement. Teaching students to identify and apply force—knowing when to push or pull, in what direction, and with what magnitude—accelerates learning and improves technical precision.

Instructors should first teach students about the mechanical concept of force before delving into specific techniques. By doing so, students gain a deeper understanding of how their actions affect their opponent and become more effective practitioners. They learn to visualise the force behind each movement and identify the key points of application in both their own techniques and in countering their opponent's.

Conclusion: Force as the Foundation

Every martial art technique, whether it's a strike, throw, or lock, is based on applying forces to change the opponent's motion or to deform their body. By simplifying the analysis into pushes and pulls, and points of application, we can better understand the mechanics behind each move, leading to clearer instruction, faster learning, and more effective techniques. Whether you're a student or an instructor, taking the time to visualise and understand the forces at play will elevate your practice, helping you master both the how and the why of martial arts.

References
Gracie, R. and R. Gracie. 2001. Brazilian Jiu-Jitsu: Theory and Technique. Montpelier, Vermont: Invisible Cities.
Kano, J. 1986. Kodokan Judo. Tokyo: Kodansha International.

John Coles holds the rank of sandan in jujutsu, shodan in aikido, and third grade in pencak silat under Jan de Jong. Training since 1983 he started teaching for Jan de Jong in 1985. Coles has since taught internationally. He is the author of *Jan de Jong: The Man, His School and His Ju Jitsu System*, authored articles published in Blitz Australasian Martial Arts and maintains two blogs: *Kojutsukan: The Place for the Study of Martial Arts Skills* and *The School of Jan de Jong*. This article is based on a chapter from his forthcoming book, *The Science Behind All Fighting Techniques*.

Issues Facing Women in Today's Martial Arts

by Maria Francis

As the world grows more aware of gender equality and inclusivity, the martial arts community has also been facing the challenge of addressing issues that affect women. Martial arts have a lot to offer to women, including personal protection and self-confidence. However, there are still underlying problems that prevent women from fully enjoying and participating in this discipline. This article aims to identify five issues that impact female martial artists and provide solutions on how to combat them. While the martial arts community has traditionally been male-dominated, there is a growing movement towards inclusivity and gender equality. By addressing these five common issues affecting female martial artists, we can make significant progress towards creating a more welcoming and supportive environment for women in the martial arts world. Martial arts are not just about physical strength and skill; they also require emotional and mental toughness. Unfortunately, women often face additional challenges in developing these qualities, especially in martial arts that involve contact and combat. As a female martial arts practitioner, I have experienced firsthand some of these issues and would like to offer some personal insights that may help in tackling them.

Gender Stereotyping
Despite growing social awareness about gender roles, gender stereotypes still persist in the martial arts community. Women are often seen as inferior fighters or less capable than men. This attitude can manifest in several ways, like assumptions that women only train for fitness or self-defence rather than competition or sparring.

Combatting gender stereotyping requires a collective effort from everyone involved in the martial arts community. One way to do this is by promoting inclusive language in dojos and gyms, avoiding gendered labels or assumptions. Coaches should also evaluate female students based on their true capabilities, rather than gender stereotypes. In addition, increasing the visibility of female martial artists through events and competitions can help break down the stigma of male dominance in the sport.

Sexual Harassment
Sexual harassment remains an issue in many martial arts gyms and dojos, often perpetuated by male instructors or fellow students. This can create a toxic environment for female martial artists and potentially prevent them from continuing with their training.
To combat sexual harassment, martial arts gyms and dojos should have strict policies in place to safeguard female students' safety. Instructors need to be held accountable for their actions, and students should be educated on consent and what constitutes sexual harassment. It's also important to ensure that female students feel comfortable reporting any incidents of harassment without fear of retaliation or judgement.

Lack of Representation
Women are underrepresented in the martial arts community, with most events and competitions dominated by men. This can lead to feelings of isolation or discouragement among female martial artists.

To address the lack of representation, it's crucial to increase female participation in martial arts events and competitions. This can be achieved by providing more opportunities for women to compete and showcasing female athletes' achievements through media and online platforms. Martial arts schools should also actively recruit more female students, including those from underserved communities.

Female martial artists often face unequal pay compared to their male counterparts in competitions and events. This can demoralise and discourage women from pursuing a career in martial arts.

Body Image Issues
The pressure to maintain a certain body type or meet specific physical standards can be a significant obstacle for women in the martial arts community. Many female martial artists feel self-conscious about their bodies or believe that they have to meet unrealistic ideals to be taken seriously as fighters.

To combat this issue, it's essential to promote a healthy body image and encourage women to focus on strength and ability rather than appearance. This can be achieved through education and awareness campaigns aimed at combating the negative stereotypes surrounding body image in martial arts. It's also important for coaches and instructors to create a positive training environment that celebrates all body types and abilities.

Fear of Intimidation
Many women hesitate to join martial arts classes because they fear being intimidated or judged by their male counterparts. They may feel uncomfortable with close physical contact or worry about standing out as the only woman in the class.

To combat this issue, instructors should ensure that classes are welcoming to everyone and that female students know they will be valued members of the dojo or gym. They should also provide women-only classes or designated training times for female students to train together without feeling self-conscious or overwhelmed.

Menstruation-Related Issues
Martial arts training can be challenging for women during their periods, especially if they
experience heavy bleeding or cramping. This can make it difficult to perform certain moves or train with intensity.

To address this issue, female martial artists can plan their training schedule around their menstrual cycle. Coaches should also be aware of the potential challenges women face during menstruation and provide appropriate accommodations. Female athletes should be encouraged to speak up about their needs and allowed to take breaks as necessary.

Pregnancy and Postpartum Training

Women who are pregnant or have recently given birth may feel unsure about continuing their martial arts training due to concerns about safety or discomfort. They may also face pressure to conform to societal expectations about what pregnancy or postpartum recovery "should" look like.

To combat this issue, martial arts schools should provide resources and support for pregnant and postpartum female athletes. This could include modifications to training routines, access to prenatal or postpartum fitness programs, and coaching on safe sparring and grappling techniques. Importantly, women should be encouraged to listen to their bodies and
make adjustments to their training based on their individual needs and limitations during pregnancy and postpartum recovery.

Lack of Female Role Models

Female martial artists often struggle to find mentors or role models they can relate to, especially if they are the only woman in their class or gym. This can make it difficult to stay motivated or inspired. To combat this issue, martial arts schools should actively seek out female instructors or coaches to provide mentorship and guidance to female students. They should also encourage female students to connect with other female martial artists through online communities or social media groups dedicated to women in martial arts.

Family and Caregiving Responsibilities

Many women in the martial arts community face additional challenges due to their roles as caregivers or family members. This may include difficulty balancing training with childcare responsibilities or feeling guilty about taking time away from their families for competitions or events.

To combat this issue, martial arts schools should provide resources and support for female athletes juggling caregiving responsibilities. This could include on-site childcare options or flexible training schedules that accommodate women's caregiving commitments. Women should also be encouraged to prioritize self-care and take the time they need to train and compete without feeling guilty or ashamed. Coaches and instructors should also recognize and respect the additional responsibilities that female athletes may face and provide support whenever possible.

While there are still challenges facing female martial artists, there are solutions available to overcome these obstacles. By promoting inclusivity, providing resources and accommodations, and highlighting the achievements of female martial artists, we can create a more supportive environment for women in the martial arts community. Through collective effort and continued education, we can work towards creating a future where all individuals have an equal opportunity to participate and excel in martial arts.

Mindfulness: Sharpening the Mind's Edge

In the world of martial arts, we often focus on the physical aspects of training - the punches, kicks, throws, and locks that form the backbone of our practice. But ask any seasoned martial artist, and they'll tell you that the mental game is just as crucial, if not more so. Enter mindfulness: a practice that's been gaining traction in recent years, not just in the wellness community, but increasingly in martial arts dojos across Australia and beyond.

What is Mindfulness?
Before we dive into how mindfulness can revolutionise your martial arts training, let's get clear on what we're talking about. Mindfulness, in its essence, is the practice of being fully present and engaged in the current moment, aware of our thoughts and feelings without getting caught up in them or judging them.

Dr. Sarah Chen, a sports psychologist who works with martial artists in Sydney, explains it this way: "Mindfulness is about training your attention. It's learning to focus on what's happening right now, rather than getting lost in worries about the future or regrets about the past. In martial arts, this translates to being fully present in your training, aware of your body, your opponent, and your surroundings."

It's important to note that mindfulness isn't about emptying your mind or achieving some blissed-out state. Rather, it's about developing a keen awareness of what's happening both internally and externally, moment by moment.

The Mindfulness-Martial Arts Connection
At first glance, the connection between mindfulness and martial arts might not be obvious. After all, isn't martial arts about action, while mindfulness is about sitting still and meditating?

Not quite, says Sensei David Thompson, a 6th Dan black belt in Karate who runs a dojo in Melbourne. "Martial arts, at its core, is about cultivating awareness," he explains. "When you're sparring, you need to be acutely aware of your opponent's movements, your own body position, the space around you. That's mindfulness in action."

The truth is, mindfulness and martial arts have more in common than you might think:

1. Focus: Both practices emphasise the importance of concentration and attention.

2. Present-moment awareness: In both mindfulness and martial arts, being fully engaged in the present moment is crucial.

3. Non-judgmental observation: Mindfulness teaches us to observe our thoughts and feelings without getting caught up in them, while martial arts training often involves observing and responding to an opponent's movements without emotional reaction.

4. Mind-body connection:
Both practices emphasise the integration of mental and physical aspects.

Incorporating mindfulness into your martial arts practice can yield a wide range of benefits:

Improved Focus and Concentration
"When I started practicing mindfulness, I noticed a significant improvement in my ability to focus during training," says Sarah Nguyen, a Brazilian Jiu-Jitsu purple belt from Brisbane. "I found myself getting distracted less and picking up techniques more quickly."

Mindfulness exercises can help train your brain to stay focused for longer periods, which is invaluable when learning complex techniques or preparing for grading.

Better Stress Management
Martial arts training can be physically and mentally demanding. Mindfulness techniques can help you manage stress more effectively, both on and off the mat.

"I use mindfulness techniques before competitions to calm my nerves," shares Mike Chen, a Taekwondo athlete from Perth. "It helps me stay centred and perform at my best under pressure."

Enhanced Body Awareness
Mindfulness practice often involves body scan exercises, where you systematically focus your attention on different parts of your body. This can translate to improved proprioception - your sense of where your body is in space - which is crucial in martial arts.

Faster Reaction Times
By training yourself to be more present and aware, you may find that your reaction times improve. This can be a significant advantage in sparring or self-defence situations.

Emotional Regulation
Mindfulness can help you develop a greater awareness of your emotional states and learn to respond rather than react impulsively. This is particularly useful in martial arts, where keeping a cool head is often crucial.

So, how can you start incorporating mindfulness into your martial arts training? Here are some practical strategies:

Implementing Mindfulness in Your Martial Arts Practice

Mindful Warm-ups

Instead of going through your warm-up routine on autopilot, try bringing mindful attention to each movement. Feel the stretch in your muscles, the rhythm of your breath, the contact of your feet with the floor.

"We start each class with a brief mindfulness exercise," says Sifu Lisa Wong, who teaches Wing Chun in Adelaide. "It helps students transition from their busy days and get focused for training."

Breath Awareness

Many martial arts already incorporate breath work, but you can take this further by regularly checking in with your breath during training. Notice its pace and depth, especially during intense exercises or sparring.

Body Scan Meditation

This can be particularly useful at the end of a training session. Lie down or sit comfortably, and systematically bring your attention to each part of your body, noticing any sensations without trying to change them.

Mindful Observation

During partner work, take a moment to really observe your training partner. Notice their stance, their breathing, the look in their eyes. This can help you become more attuned to subtle cues that might telegraph their next move.

Present-Moment Focus

When learning a new technique, bring your full attention to each aspect of the movement. Notice the placement of your feet, the alignment of your hips, the position of your hands. This level of attention can help you pick up nuances you might otherwise miss.

Use the cool-down period at the end of training to practice mindfulness. As you stretch, pay attention to the sensations in your body, your gradually slowing breath, and the feeling of relaxation spreading through your muscles.

While the benefits of mindfulness in martial arts are clear, implementing it isn't always easy. Here are some common challenges and how to address them:

1. "I don't have time for mindfulness"
Remember, mindfulness doesn't always mean sitting in meditation for long periods. "You can practice mindfulness in short bursts throughout your training," advises Dr. Chen. "Even 30 seconds of focused attention on your breath can make a difference."

2. "My mind keeps wandering"
This is completely normal and part of the process. The key is to gently bring your attention back to the present moment whenever you notice your mind has wandered, without judging yourself.

3. "I feel silly doing it"
Some students might feel self-conscious about practicing mindfulness, especially in a group setting. Start with simple, subtle practices like breath awareness, which you can do without anyone noticing.

4. "I'm not seeing immediate results"
Like any skill, mindfulness takes time to develop. "Stick with it," encourages Sensei Thompson. "The benefits might be subtle at first, but they compound over time."

Mindfulness Beyond the Dojo
One of the great things about mindfulness is that its benefits extend far beyond your martial arts practice. Many martial artists find that the mindfulness skills they develop in training help them in other areas of life, from work to relationships.

"The mindfulness I've learned through martial arts has made me a better teacher," says Jonathan Smith, a high school teacher and Judo brown belt from Hobart. "I'm more patient, more present with my students, and better able to handle the stress of the job."

Moreover, the combination of physical exercise and mindfulness practice in martial arts can be a powerful tool for overall mental health and wellbeing.

The Future of Mindfulness in Martial Arts

As awareness of the benefits of mindfulness grows, we're likely to see it becoming an increasingly integral part of martial arts training. Some dojos are already incorporating formal mindfulness instruction into their curricula.

"I believe mindfulness will become as fundamental to martial arts training as physical conditioning," predicts Dr. Chen. "The martial artists who can master both the physical and mental aspects will be the ones who truly excel."

In the end, the goal of incorporating mindfulness into martial arts isn't to change the essence of your practice, but to enhance it. By training your mind alongside your body, you can take your martial arts journey to new heights.

Remember, like any aspect of martial arts training, developing mindfulness is a journey, not a destination. There will be days when it feels easy and natural, and others when it's a struggle. The key is to approach it with the same patience, persistence, and dedication you bring to your physical training.

As the ancient samurai saying goes, "The mind is everything. What you think, you become." By cultivating mindfulness in your martial arts practice, you're not just becoming a better fighter - you're becoming a more aware, centred, and balanced human being. And in today's fast-paced, often chaotic world, that might be the most valuable skill of all.

Write for Us

We want your authentic story, your journey and the reason WHY you love what you do. Below is a list of suggested topics. It is not exhaustive, so if you have an idea that we haven't come up with yet, drop us a line: training tips; technique workshops; style origins;kids in ma; training fuel; style anatomy; family pages; instructor profile; keeping it real; and more...

We are a quarterly magazine that celebrates and inspires a broad community of Martial Artists across the country. Our goal is to support all MA practitioners. Both instructors and students are encouraged to share their personal experiences, triumphs, and challenges within the style they love.

We feature interviews, rants, research, photography, projects and editorials that are respectful to all styles and are keeping in line with our magazine's inclusive philosophy.

Just as no two styles of Martial Arts are alike, our writers should have their own unique voice and tell their story from their own perspective. We encourage you to speak your truth.

Don't worry if you feel that your writing is not up to scratch, just tell us your story, your tip or your instruction the best way you can and our in-house editor will do the rest.

Email your submissions to info@martialartsmagazineaustralia.com (text in .doc) and (photos in JPEG).

www.ingramcontent.com/pod-product-compliance
Lightning Source LLC
Chambersburg PA
CBHW051512100526
44585CB00043B/2469